I0472033

THE DIGITALLY LITERATE CITIZEN

HOW DIGITAL LITERACY EMPOWERS MASS PARTICIPATION IN THE UNITED STATES

A Masters Thesis
By **Jeremy J. Riel**

Lulu Publishing
www.lulu.com

i

This book is a printing of the Masters Thesis completed and defended by the author at Georgetown University. The text printed within is identical to the final submission of the thesis to the Graduate School of Arts and Sciences and department of Communication, Culture and Technology.

Washington, D.C.
April 23, 2012

ISBN: 978-1-105-84311-2

Cover image by Jeremy Riel
"high tech, low tech"
From CCTP 506, Fundamentals of Technology
Communication, Culture and Technology Department
Georgetown University

Published by Lulu
www.lulu.com

THE DIGITALLY LITERATE CITIZEN: HOW DIGITAL LITERACY EMPOWERS MASS PARTICIPATION IN THE UNITED STATES

Jeremy Riel, B.A.

Thesis Advisor: Diana M. Owen, Ph.D.

ABSTRACT

From online political campaigning to Internet social clubs, the American mass participation environment has become increasingly mediated by digital technologies or tools. From social membership in groups and clubs to political participation to influencing government action, information technologies have become popular for expressing ideas and building social capital. In this thesis, I argue that digital literacy, or the ability to use electronic tools to retrieve, evaluate, and create information, has become essential for engagement in various mass participation and social activities in the United States, including those activities within the domains of social membership, civic, political, and online participation. Because of the increased use of information technologies in the public sphere, technology and information skills have become required to effectively participate socially and politically. Using data from a nationally representative survey, I illustrate several findings that indicate the strength of digital literacy skills in empowering public for social membership participation, political participation, and online social activities.

KEYWORDS

Digital literacy; information literacy; media literacy; technology skills; mass participation; political participation; civic participation; digital divide

iii

TABLE OF CONTENTS

LIST OF FIGURES

LIST OF TABLES

CHAPTER 1 - INTRODUCTION

From fundamental changes to election campaigns to the development of computer-mediated democracy, digital technologies have greatly influenced the ways in which people interact with their families, friends, communities, and governments. However, advances in digital technologies have also changed the required skills for communicating and gathering information. As the Internet and other networked applications became integrated into mainstream avenues for mass participation, it is likely that the mass participation environment now requires people to be digitally literate. In this thesis, I explore this claim by analyzing the influence that digital literacy skills have on several domains of mass participation, including social membership, civic, political, and online participation.

My goal for this thesis is to identify digital literacy skills that have become necessary for mass participation in the United States and the degree of influence they have on participation. Defined, digital literacy is the ability to efficiently use electronic, networked tools to find, evaluate, create, distribute, and synthesize electronically mediated information. Mass participation is defined as engagement in social, civic, and political activities. Generally, mass participation includes activities to socialize, to influence others' behaviors and attitudes, or to effect social or political change, such as encouraging someone to give

1

money to a cause or petitioning a public official toward a particular policy decision. In this thesis, I argue that digital literacy skills are essential for people to influence political change or to socialize today. In addition, I argue that expressive digital skills, such as digital publication, sharing, and multimedia skills, empower people to become engaged the most when compared to other types of digital skills. By analyzing data from a survey developed for this thesis, I demonstrate that digital literacy is a strong predictor of mass participation in its various forms and has become an antecedent skill that empowers the public to engage in the modern participation environment.

While much of the past research on mass participation activity has focused on certain antecedent skills and preconditions that are required for the public to become engaged, few studies have deeply explored whether digital literacy is required for mass participation in the Internet Age. Aside from anecdotal evidence that is frequently provided by news pundits, educators, elected officials, and other social commentators on the lack of technology and information skills of the public, the literature lacks sufficient empirical data that reflects the influence that digital literacy has on the abilities of Americans to participate and perform civic functions. I was encouraged to perform this research by wondering if whether some groups of people are being left out of the public sphere because of their lack of digital skills. Also, I wondered if digital literacy skills really mattered that much in a person's participation behaviors, or if traditionally held preconditions, such as available time or money, someone's strength of political ideology, and social demographics, were more important to determining someone's level of mass participation.

Because digital literacy is a novel concept and because of the large amount of theoretical work that has been recently performed in this area by scholars, this thesis is just as much about understanding digital literacy as it is about how digital literacy influencess American civic life and participatory behavior. To guide this thesis, I ask the following primary research question: To what degree is digital literacy a predictor of mass participation? Because of the rapid development of technology, it is increasingly difficult to pinpoint changes to technologies and how they are used by various groups of people. As such, I also ask the following questions to guide the construction of the research instruments that I use in this thesis: What digital literacy skills are used in daily life? Are any digital literacy skills required for mass participation (i.e., are antecedent to participation)?

1.1 – FRAMEWORK AND PAST RESEARCH

I draw from two primary subject areas to provide the framework for this thesis. First, I perform a comprehensive review of the past research in mass participation from the communications and political science disciplines. Second, in order to gain an understanding of the developing relationship of digital literacy to mass participation, I review literature from the education and literary studies disciplines and the recent theoretical work on the concept of digital literacy skills. This literature also explores the trends surrounding emergent digital skills, how traditional notions of literacy have expanded due to the advent of information technologies, and how society has been influenced by this shift.

Scholars have linked various types of political and civic activities to life experiences or levels of socioeconomic status, while having simultaneously developed detailed typologies of political and civic participation (Conway, 1985; Milbrath 1965; Verba, Schlozman, & Brady, 1995; Verba and Nie, 1972). The measures of mass participation that have been used by scholars have grown to become highly specified models that distinguish between political, civic, and social membership participation. Participation in the political domain is often linked to the civic participation domain (Zukin, Keter, Andolina, Jenkins, & Delli Carpini, 2006).

In conjunction with studying the levels of mass participation among the public, scholars have also measured the influence of various antecedent conditions or required resources for participation. One example of an antecedent precondition is access to influence or technology. During the early years of the Internet, people without access to digital technologies were associated with lower levels of participation (Norris, 2001; Warschauer, 2003; Van Dijk 2005). Also, those with more time, money, or social influence were more likely to engage in mass participation activities (Conway, 1985; Verba, Schlozman, & Brady, 1995; Lijphart, 1997; Schattschneider, 1960). Another example of an antecedent condition for participation is political and civic knowledge, as those with higher levels of knowledge of political and civic affairs demonstrate higher levels of participation (Galston, 2001; Delli Carpini & Keter 1996; Milner, 2002; Prior, 2005,

2007). Civic education programs that aim to increase knowledge also result in higher levels of mass participation (Finkel, 2003; Niemi & Junn, 1998). Finally, literacy and communication skills have been linked to higher levels of mass participation (Sen, 1992; Streck, 1998; Wilhelm, 2000). Literacy skills, which are part of a larger set of "civic skills," or the ability to communicate effectively in public contexts, have been found to be strong antecedent skills for participation (Brady, Verba, & Schlozman, 1995).

As broadcast media became prominent in America, scholars have increasingly associated mass media use to lower levels of mass participation and higher levels of social isolation (Putnam, 2000; Conway, 1985). However, with the rise of the Internet as a platform for social interaction, scholars have found that the Internet does not necessarily isolate users, but instead fosters the development of digitally mediated communities with new types of participation as a result (Katz & Rice, 2002; Putnam & Feldstein, 2003; Zukin, et al., 2006). Largely because of the increased ability to gather information and connect with other people, scholars suggest that a new form of citizenship has emerged, which values closely monitoring civic and political issues and not necessarily becoming engaged until it becomes necessary (Schudson, 1999; Zukin, et al., 2006; Oldenburg 1999; Rheingold, 1993).

This increasingly mediated participatory environment has allowed for specialization of interests and for a new level of social monitoring that was more difficult in years past (Schudson, 1999; Negroponte, 1995). However, this environment has also demonstrated an increase in the complexity of information analysis and technical skills required to receive balanced and accurate information with which to make decisions (Sunstein, 2007; Jamieson & Cappella, 2008; Stroud, 2011). New skills that expand the notion of traditional literacy are needed in order to navigate and interpret the large amounts of digital information within various multimedia applications.

Scholars argue that competency with digital technologies is important for a robust civic life (Tyner, 1998; Gee, 2008; Martin, 2010). Because digital technologies present language in a variety of ways through multimedia and electronic representation, there are also multiple ways in which digital texts can be created and interpreted. Digital literacy scholars suggest that a digitally literate person should not only know how to operate the technology, but should also understand the social contexts under which information is created and the limits of the media in which information is presented (Gee, 2008; Lankshear & Knobel, 2006; Gilster, 1997; Street, 1995; Kress, 2003; Cope & Kalantzis, 2000). In light of this, measures of digital literacy should not only include mastery of discrete technological skills, but also a broader understanding of the origins and bias of information.

In my review of the literature on digital literacy, I identified six domains of skills that were frequently noted by digital literacy theorists. Foundational *computer skills* provide the technical basis for the use of any information technologies and are generally required for any higher-order digital literacy mastery (Jenkins, 2006a; International Technology Education Association, 2002; Trilling & Fadel, 2009). *Information skills* address the theoretical assumption that users of information technologies should also be able to critically acquire, analyze, and use information efficiently. Scholars argue that without information skills, users of information technologies will be unable to make sense of the deluge of information that is available to users (Gilster, 1997; Rushkoff, 2010; Bawden, 2001; Snavely & Cooper, 1997).

The domains of *communication skills* (the ability to send and receive information) and *publication skills* (the ability to create information) address the delivery and sharing functions that information technologies provide. Scholars hold that the ability to properly interpret messages within various media, choose the proper medium for communication or expression, and to combine media for various effects are essential for a digitally literate person (Jenkins, 2006b; Tyner, 1998; Hobbs, 1998; Buckingham, 2003; Wilde & Wilde, 1991). *Innovative thinking skills*, which include critical thinking, an experimental attitude, and a history of creativity and customization with technology are also regarded as necessary for the digitally literate person. Innovative thinking skills enable flexibility when learning new technologies and provide mental models for creating custom uses of technology to meet one's needs (Jenkins, 2006a; American Association for the Advancement of Science, 1990). Finally, digital literacy scholars find that *cultural and historical knowledge* on technology issues aid a person in anticipating the consequences of his or her technology use and help inform his or her choice of media (Pearson & Young, 2002; Jenkins, 2006a; Trilling & Fadel, 2009; Rushkoff, 2010). These knowledge areas include legal issues with technology, intellectual property, online privacy, the risks and benefits of technology, and current technology trends.

The six domains of digital literacy that I identify in this thesis all benefit a person's ability for self-expression and conveyance of ideas or social needs. Complimenting the traditional notion of literacy as the ability to read and write, this expanded notion of digital literacy accounts for the virtually unlimited number of combinations of media with which a person can use information technology to communicate and interpret language. This multimodal view of literacy has become an antecedent skill that is required for many forms of mass participation. In effect, these skills represent a new set of civic skills that empower the public to have a robust social life and community connection.

1.2 – HYPOTHESES AND METHODS

To examine the influence of digital literacy on various forms of mass participation, I have developed the following hypotheses that will be tested in this thesis:

H_1: Knowledge of cultural and historical issues of technology is correlated the most with higher levels of mass participation when compared to the other five domains of digital literacy

H_2: Digital literacy skills that are used for creativity and content publication are correlated with higher levels mass participation when compared to computer, information, and communication skills

H₃: Digital literacy is the strongest predictor of traditional mass participation when compared to strength of political ideology and social demographics

H₄: Online participation is influenced the most by digital literacy skills when compared across the four domains of mass participation

H₅: Higher levels of digital literacy predict higher levels of political participation

I perform a series of statistical analyses to test these hypotheses, including Pearson's R correlations and ordinary least-square (OLS) regressions. These statistical procedures use data from the 2012 Technology Use Survey, which provide information on respondent levels of digital literacy as measured by 59 indicators of skill and knowledge. In addition, the survey provides data on respondent levels of mass participation in four domains, which include social membership, civic, political, and online participation. To measure levels of digital literacy and mass participation in the various domains, I developed several indexes from the survey indicators. Each index showed high levels of statistical reliability.

1.3 - FINDINGS

The hypothesis tests in this thesis provide multiple layers of evidence that indicates the presence of digital literacy as an antecedent skill for mass participation. First, I found that knowledge of cultural and historical issues related to technology and digital literacy skills used for creativity and publication were the most influential on participation activities. This finding indicated that the ability to share ideas and create digital content while understanding the social contexts under which that content is shared empowers engagement in the electronically mediated participation environment. Second, I found that digital literacy is the strongest predictor of traditional mass participation when compared to several control variables including strength of political ideology and socioeconomic status. Third, when comparing differences between the four domains of mass participation, I found that higher levels of digital literacy significantly predicted higher levels of participation three domains: social membership, political, and online participation. On the other hand, digital literacy was not predictive of high levels of civic participation domain, which indicates that digital technologies are not as important for participation in this domain. For the other three domains of participation, these findings show how digital technologies have become ubiquitous and the importance of digital skills for participants.

This thesis contributes to the understanding of both digital literacy and mass participation in several ways. Primarily, my findings illustrate the growing importance of digital skills to the mass participation environment. Second, digital literacy is demonstrated to be antecedent skill that influences mass participation. It joins the several other preconditions that have already been know to predetermine engagement, which include civic and political knowledge, money, time, strength of ideology, exposure to information and media, and socialization (Wilhelm, 2000; Zukin, et al,

2006; Brady, Verba, Schlozman, 1995). Finally, this thesis contributes a new model for measuring digital literacy through the use of several indicators and indexes. These measures can assist with the development of more robust metrics for digital literacy in future research.

1.4 – ORGANIZATION OF THE THESIS

The thesis is divided into seven chapters, including this one. In Chapter 2, I perform a comprehensive literature review of past research of mass participation behaviors and attitudes, preconditions and skills that are required for participation, and the emergence of digital literacy skills. In this chapter, I also discuss my theoretical framework, research questions, and formal hypotheses. In Chapter 3, I provide a detailed description of the methods used in the study, the manner in which I collected data with the 2012 Technology Use Survey, how the primary measures were constructed for the thesis (which include indexes for digital literacy and mass participation), and the statistical methods that were used to test the hypotheses. Chapter 4 provides a brief descriptive analysis of the survey respondents, indicating the general levels of digital literacy skills held by the public. These are also divided and compared by gender and age. In addition, the participation levels of the public within the four domains of mass participation are described in this chapter and are compared by gender and age. In Chapter 5, I formally test the research hypotheses using OLS regression and correlation methodology. This chapter provides a step-by-step walkthrough of the data analysis. In Chapter 6, I synthesize the findings from the hypotheses and statistical analyses, discuss these findings in detail, and provide several possible explanations for the results. Chapter 7 summarizes the study and its findings, as well as the potential impact the thesis could have on various organizations or social institutions.

CHAPTER 2: LITERATURE REVIEW AND THEORETICAL FRAMEWORK

Mass participation is frequently regarded as the currency with which a healthy democracy operates. Since the founding of the republic, the public sphere has been a marketplace of transformative ideas that have guided America to where it is today. Given today's complex communication technologies, the number of opportunities for participation has dramatically expanded since the days of America's founding. The proliferation of digital tools that are used for mass participation has likely brought about a new set of prerequisite skills and knowledge with which the public must be familiar. This rise in complexity of information technology has also created a difficulty in accurately assessing the degree by which the participation landscape has changed alongside the development of information technology.

The expansion of digital technologies into the realm of mass participation has encouraged volumes of research over the last twenty years. Much of this research explores the types of activities in which the public engages, the types of media used with participation, and the various social factors that encourage participation. This body of research has explored how various forms of public involvement influence social institutions and policy. The literature also explores the types of knowledge and prerequisite skills that are required for influential and informed mass participation. With this dramatic change to the participation landscape parallel to the rapid development of information technologies, the preconditions for participation could be changing just as rapidly. These rules can include various antecedent skills, knowledge, and points of access that are required for participation. As mass participation has taken new shape as a result of information technology use, the antecedent skills and knowledge that are required for mass participation have likely shifted as well.

In this thesis, I examine the degree to which digital literacy is an antecedent skill for mass participation in the Internet Age. Digital literacy, defined as the ability to efficiently use electronic, networked tools to find, evaluate, create, distribute and synthesize electronically mediated information, is frequently regarded by education and literary scholars as an emerging skill set for the general public. Can the possession of digital literacy predict involvement in the public sphere? Does digital literacy provide more effective avenues to gain community membership, voice social grievances, or exercise socioeconomic influence? With the ubiquity of digital technologies in modern society, these new form of literacy skills are increasingly required for participation.

The study of digital literacy as a skill for mass participation can illustrate who is using digital skills, how digital skills are used for mass participation, and the types of barriers associated with acquiring digital literacy skills. In addition, the possession or lack of digital literacy skills in relation to participation could illustrate social ramifications for various demographics. Findings in this area also reveal some of the possibilities for deliberative democracies in the 21st century. These findings highlight the promises and challenges associated with the use of networked technologies for mass participation. As demonstrated by various technology-powered social movements around the world, such as the American Tea Party, the 2011-2012 Occupy Wall Street movement, and the 2011 Arab Spring, democratic and non-democratic societies alike are re-negotiating the interplay between technology, social institutions, and socioeconomic influence.

In this chapter, I highlight past literature on mass participation, antecedent skills and preconditions for participation, description of digital literacy theory, and its relationship to mass participation. First, I explore the concept of mass participation and define the four domains of participation that this thesis will analyze. Second, I review the history of mass participation research in the United States to get a glimpse of how mass participation research has become highly detailed in describing the types of people who get involved in various public activities, especially in the wake of the development of the Internet and other digital tools. Next, I examine past work that identifies antecedent preconditions and skills that have been found to predict a person's level of mass participation. Finally, I explore the concept of digital literacy and position it within the current literature on antecedent skills and preconditions for mass participation. Digital literacy has developed from the traditional notion of literacy, which has been expanded by the exponential growth of information technologies. As digital literacy is a new antecedent skill, the possession of digital literacy skills among the public could be a new indicator of social influence as it is exercised through participation.

2.1 – MASS PARTICIPATION DEFINED

Mass participation activities have enjoyed a rich history of research and discussion. I define I define mass participation as engagement in social, civic, and political activities. Generally, mass participation includes activities to socialize, to influence others' behaviors and attitudes, or to effect social or political change, such as encouraging someone to give money to a cause or petitioning a public official toward a particular policy decision. As illustrated in Table 2.1, I analyze four domains of mass participation in this thesis: political participation, civic participation, social membership participation, and online participation. Each of the four domains is associated with specific goals and activities.

**Four Domains of Mass
Participation**

1. *Political Participation*

2. *Civic Participation*

3. *Social Membership Participation*

4. *Online Participation*

Table 2.1

Four Domains of Mass Participation

Perhaps the most researched domain of mass participation is *political participation*. Verba, Schlozman, and Brady (1995) and Zukin, et al. (2006) define political participation as "activity that has the intent or effect of influencing government action – either directly by affecting the making or implementation of public policy, or indirectly by influencing the selection of people who make those policies" (pp. 6). Activities such as voting, donating to political candidates, contacting public officials, and political club membership are all distinct, measurable forms of political participation (Putnam, 2000, pp. 35-46). In addition, Zukin, et al. (2006) identify the concept of *public voice* in political participation activities, which are indirect efforts to influence political outcomes through the discussion or sharing of political issues through various media with other members of the public. All of these

17

activities are included in my measures of political participation as described in Chapter 3.

Although scholars have linked it to political participation, *civic participation* is a distinct category of activity from political participation (Verba, Schlozman, & Brady, 1995; Putnam, 2000; Zukin, et al., 2006). Civic participation is not aimed at influencing government action and is usually associated with a high degree of volunteerism or service to others. As defined by Zukin, et al, civic engagement is "organized voluntary activity focused on problem solving and helping others. It includes a wide range of work undertaken alone or in concert with others to effect change" (2006, pp. 7). I use this definition for civic participation in this thesis as it includes volunteerism, philanthropy, or other overt efforts to influence social policy or situations. These activities, while separate from those of political participation, also seek outcomes that influence social situations. As such, this domain of participation is an important one regarding the research of mass participation, even though some scholars argue that political participation might be more important for the democratic health (Zukin, et al., 2006).

While not necessarily promoting social change or solving problems, some forms of mass participation can increase a person's social capital that can then be used for civic participation (Putnam, 2000, pp. 116). The types of community activities that do not express a clear intent to solve problems or help others but still serve to connect people, build social capital, or are used for personal satisfaction or growth are classified under what I call the *social membership participation* domain. Social membership participation is defined as in-person, voluntary activity in which an individual takes part in or shares in activities for personal growth and common interests, but does not necessarily seek the social change or problem-solving outcomes demonstrated by activities in the civic participation domain. Activities within the social membership participation domain include joining clubs, organizations, hobby groups, or other membership-oriented groups. In addition to civic participation and social service, a robust social life is helpful for improving not only the individual but also the community in which they interact (Oldenburg, 1999). While many groups might serve to solve problems and meet outcomes, the benefit to the individual and the community is present through both personal and external community benefits that can enrich the communities with which individuals interact, thereby adding to civic vibrancy (Putnam, 2000).

Similar to the types of activity in the social membership participation domain, *online participation* has become an emergent avenue for social activity as the Internet increasingly serves as a medium for interpersonal communication and organization. Digital communication platforms afford the opportunity for real-time sharing, cross-geographical connection, and meaningful exchange that can empower social life and public discourse (Rheingold, 1993; Jenkins, 2006b; Katz & Rice, 2002; Coleman & Blumler, 2009). As such, some social activities may occur exclusively on digital platforms. Although similar to the social membership participation domain mentioned above, I define online participation as voluntary activity in which an individual takes part in or shares in activities for personal growth and common interests, but does so solely via networked electronic communications. Activities in this domain include participation in online games, Internet message boards and forums, online dating, and other communities for sharing information that are mediated solely via the Internet.

To summarize, American mass participation exhibits multiple domains of activities that range from local social interaction to high group membership with millions of members and large infrastructures. Participants in these activities have various goals that range from the fulfilling of social interaction and personal interests (such as hobbies or entertainment) to charity work to political change. To achieve these goals, participants use various skills and knowledge they have acquired either through past personal experience or their desire to participate.

2.2 – MASS PARTICIPATION RESEARCH AND MEASUREMENT

The measurement of mass participation has been of particular interest to political science, communications, and democracy scholars. Some key studies have substantially contributed to the understanding of mass participation and have led to sophisticated models for its study. Milbrath's (1965) seminal framework provided a set of parameters with which scholars could analyze political participation. This framework characterized political participation as a pyramid of activity in which people move from lower levels (voting, learning about a candidate) to higher levels of more engaged activity (volunteering for a campaign or running for office). Milbrath was one of the first scholars to use a categorized model of measured political participation to link participation with individual and external characteristics, such as socioeconomic status and life experiences. Verba and Nie (1972) established four distinct categories of political activity in which the public can engage: voting, election campaign activity, contacting public officials, and cooperative activity. In their analysis, they confirmed the high correlation of socioeconomic status to political participation. A person's race and community size were also determined to be factors that determine participation. Conway's (1985) research on political participation confirmed the same high correlation of socioeconomic and life experience patterns with civic and political participation, finding additionally that mass media use decreases trust in community institutions and reduces social interaction within communities.

Verba, Schlozman, and Brady (1995) studied the concept of civic volunteerism in addition to political participation and provided a better distinction between civic service activities and political activities. Their work found that various socioeconomic and access factors influence public levels of participation in both the civic and political realms. Putnam's (2000) famous analysis on social capital explored the behaviors of demographic groups and their activity in a variety of participation domains. After finding a great decline in levels participation in all domains from 1950 to 1990, such as in levels of membership in social organizations, Putnam attributes this drop in activity to information technologies that have individualized the American public and have encouraged an attitude of isolation, particularly through broadcast television. In a

21

future study, however, Putnam and Feldstein (2003) realize that participation levels might instead be shifting to new territory with the increase in information technologies, and not just simply disappearing as new technologies for engagement emerge.

Acknowledging the rise of the Internet as a vehicle for social communication and organization, Katz and Rice (2002) identified some implications of participation in the age of the Internet and its use on a variety of social institutions. They find that the Internet is not necessarily a tool that encourages social isolation, but instead fosters the development of new forms of communities. Schudson's (1999) review of the history of citizen participation reveals that alongside increased mediation over the years, participation has indeed changed in form and that certain activities have lessened as social trends changed. However, he also finds that the American public remains engaged and attentive in ways that compliment the demands of modern daily life. These activities often blur the boundaries between the traditionally held political and civic categories of mass participation, making it difficult to know when people are paying attention or even actively participating. The work of Zukin, et al. (2006), confirms Schudson's (1999) assertion by revealing that while levels of civic and political participation have indeed shifted over the last half-century for some specific activities, there has been a rise in new types of social organization and communication, especially when people have higher amounts of prior political and civic knowledge. This is particularly true of the younger, more digitally apt generations. Their work also illustrates the "clustering" of mass participation activities between the civic and political participation domains, making it harder to delineate clear categorical definitions (pp. 191-192). Activities have the potential to represent multiple domains, such as being "service" and "politically" oriented at the same time simultaneously. This makes it more challenging to accurately measure levels of mass participation.

2.3 – THE INFLUENCE OF DIGITAL TECHNOLOGIES ON MASS PARTICIPATION SKILLS AND PRECONDITIONS

Certain life experiences and goals, such as parental guidance, political socialization within communities, or personal gratification, have been traditionally known to influence a person's interest in mass participation. As research on mass participation broadened, scholars have identified in greater detail other preconditions and antecedent skills that influence a person's ability for and interest in mass participation. These preconditions and skills include access to technology and influence, political and civic knowledge, exposure to information, and literacy and communication skills. As the increased use of information technologies has facilitated a new participatory environment, I argue that digital literacy skills have become highly influential in empowering mass participation activities. As such, digital literacy skills should be considered as an antecedent skill set. By enabling people to use various information technology tools with which to gather and process information, digital literacy skills can also compliment the development of other antecedent skills and preconditions, such as civic and political knowledge gathering and access to information.

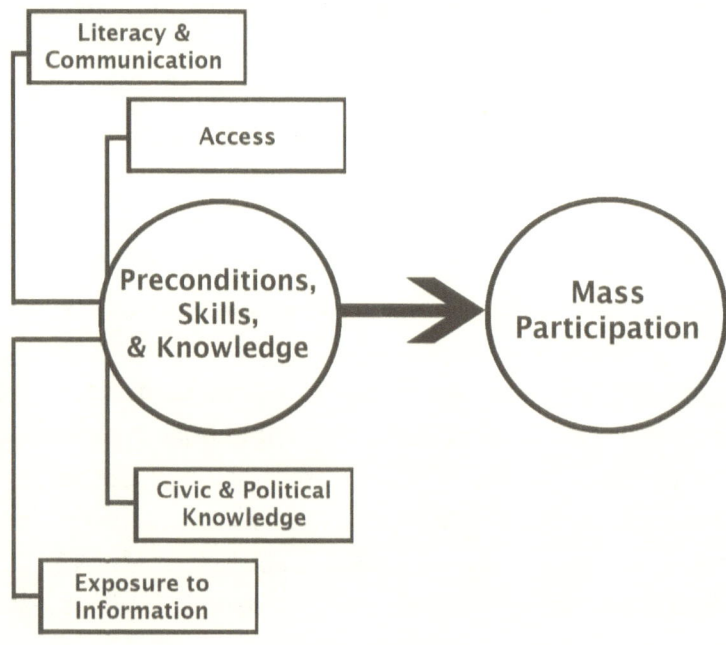

Figure 2.1
Relationship between Antecedent Resources and Mass
Participation(as reflected in past literature)

Past research has examined the presence of "resource requirements" that are necessary for mass participation, such as specific skills, preconditions, and knowledge (Wilhelm, 2000; Delli Carpini & Keter, 1993; Brady, Yerba, & Schlozman, 1995; Hargittai, 2003). Work in this field has revealed that those with higher levels of access to antecedent skills or knowledge will be more likely to participate. While participation preconditions and skills are often acquired as a result of various life experiences unrelated to a person's mass participation activities, they can also be learned as a result of an interest or desire for mass participation (Wilhelm, 2000; Verba, Schlozman, & Brady, 1995; Lijphart, 1997). Figure 2.1 illustrates the relationship of antecedent skills, preconditions, and knowledge with mass participation and how they serve to influence levels of participation.

Access to resources or influence has been a reliable predictor of mass participation for many years. Those with higher levels of available time, money, or social influence generally participate at higher levels than those who lack such resources (Conway, 1985; Schattschneider, 1960; Verba, Schlozman, Brady, 1995; Lijphart, 1997). In addition, as information technologies became increasingly integrated into mass participation activities, those without access to the technological tools for communication or media consumption are less inclined to participate (Norris, 2001; Warschauer, 2003; van Dijk, 2005). Participation within this "digital divide" environment has been regularly characterized as prohibitive to those of lower socioeconomic status due to the high cost of information technology and Internet access. However, as costs have dramatically decreased since 2000, the adoption of information technologies has exponentially increased among the public. As a result, access to technology is less of a concern today than it has been in years past and may play a lesser role in predicting mass participation. Despite this, access exists as an antecedent precondition for participation.

Political and civic knowledge is another antecedent resource that can influence mass participation. Those with higher levels of political and civic knowledge are better able to make informed decisions about their activities (Galston, 2001; Delli Carpini & Keter, 1996; Milner, 2002; Prior, 2005, 2007). Examples of civic and political knowledge include democratic process, information about political leaders or candidates, the ways to voice grievances, and knowledge of current events. Formal civic education programs have been shown to increase political and civic knowledge in participants, and, as a result, increase participation (Finkel, 2003; Niemi & Junn, 1998). Higher levels of political and civic knowledge could increase feelings of efficacy in mass participation activities as well. To extend political and civic knowledge persuasion to the digital realm, information technologies and the Internet have been used in new ways to communicate information to the public.

An illustrative example of the effects of integrating digital tools in political and civic knowledge promotion has been in the use of the political websites to inform voters and encourage engagement (Gibson and Ward, 2000; Stromer-Galley, 2000; Owen and Davis, 2008; Lupia and Philpot, 2005; Herrnson, Stokes-Brown, and Hindman, 2007; Latimer 2009). As digital technologies further developed, political websites began to employ social media and other interactive elements to encourage a variety of political participation activities. Scholars frequently find, however, that only partisans usually visit political websites, and as such, little effort is made on campaign websites to encourage uncommitted voters toward higher levels of political participation (Bimber and Davis, 2003; Foot and Schneider, 2006). This lack of involvement by non-partisans indicates that traditional activities extended into the digital realm might not be attractive or accessible to those not already possessing civic and political knowledge, which only serves to perpetuate the traditionally held influence structures. Nonpartisans might instead participate in mass participation activities in the political domain differently than how politicians and government officials have designed the participatory environment, and possibly using different technologies or applications than those intended by the political elite.

Similar to the active political and civic knowledge gathering activities mentioned above, the public's *exposure to information* is another precondition for mass participation. Zukin, et al (2006), outline this type of antecedent precondition for mass participation in what they call cognitive engagement. Cognitive engagement is the manner in which people pay attention to or are exposed to civic and political information, but don't necessarily take overt action with issues of politics and public affairs (pp. 54). Those with higher levels of exposure and attention to civic and political issues will be more inclined for participation (Delli Carpini & Keter, 1996). Schudson (1999) echoes this observation by proposing the presence of the "monitorial citizen," or a citizen that is attentive to public issues that influence his or her life in the modern American high-tech participation environment (pp. 311). The monitorial citizen doesn't take action until issues directly affect them. Instead, the monitorial citizen stays appraised of news that might affect them and is "poised for action if action is required" (pp. 311).

Information technologies have shown promise in empowering the exposure precondition, but a person would need antecedent technical and communication skills to be connected to information in the first place. New media could undermine traditional information gatekeeper roles and see the rise of a more diverse, specialized information environment that can be tailored to the individual's needs and interests (Williams & Delli Carpini, 2000; Hargittai, 2000; Negroponte, 1995). In addition, the Internet is frequently regarded as promising due to the ability to find niche interests or social causes in which they believe (Anderson, 2006).

However, after the year 2000, evidence of the use of digital tools for information exposure pointed toward grimmer outcomes. Hargittai (2003) found that in the course of political knowledge gathering activities over the Internet, the public lacked sophistication in search and information retrieval skills. This resulted in a narrower range of information that would be consumed by users, thus reducing the potential of the Web. With the ability to customize information streams, Karmark and Nye (2002) suggest that the Web could be promoting a fragmentation effect caused by the lack of broad-interest ideas in public information channels and online news media. Other scholars assert that an "echo chamber" could be created from this specialization of information streams, with the public missing out on key pieces of information that are critical to forming opinions and informing mass participation (Sunstein, 2007; Jamieson & Cappella, 2008;

Stroud, 2011; Chadwick, 2006). These scholars recognize that the ability to acquire and evaluate information from several sources is becoming an important part of mass participation and suggest that efforts to remediate these potential challenges should be employed.

Finally, *literacy and communication skills* have been found to be antecedent to mass participation (Wilhelm, 2000; Sen, 1992; Streck, 1998). The presence of these "civic skills", or the ability to communicate effectively in public contexts, has been found to influence mass participation (Brady, Verba, & Schlozman, 1995). Brady, Verba, and Schlozman measured literacy and communication skills in a mass participation context by creating an index to measure civic skills as it relates to political participation. This index included skills such as the ability to read, write, and speak as well as the ability to organize, to take part in meetings, and to work in groups. They argued that these skills positively influence a person's ability for mass participation. As new media and other digital technologies became increasingly available, however, communication skills and what it meant to be literate in the 21st Century were altered and gave rise to digital literacy. Digital literacy better specifies the style, methods, tools, and language used when communicating within digital contexts, something with which the definition of traditional literacy is not flexible enough to compliment.

2.4 – DIGITAL LITERACY AS AN ANTECEDENT SKILL

In response to the proliferation of information technologies in the public sphere, literary scholars have asserted the increasing value of digital literacy skills for mass participation (Tyner, 1998; Gee 2008; Martin, 2010). Digital literacy is defined as the ability to efficiently use electronic, networked tools to find, evaluate, create, distribute and synthesize electronically mediated information. As discussed in the above sections, scholars have illustrated an increasing need for the public to gain a mastery of technology and information processing skills. As such, several computing, information, and other technology skills that fall under the category of digital literacy have become a new antecedent skill set for mass participation. This is especially true as public institutions increase their use of information technologies, as schools integrate the teaching of these skills into the curriculum, as political campaigns are increasingly digitally mediated, and as civic discourse includes bits and bytes and not just face-to-face conversations. Figure 2.2 further illustrates digital literacy as an antecedent skill to mass participation. In this model, digital literacy works alongside other antecedent conditions and skills to influence the level of a person's mass participation. While the various antecedent preconditions and skills may influence each other, I do not assume so in this model for the sake of singling out digital literacy as an antecedent skill for study.

Digital literacy derives from the traditional concept of literacy: the ability to read and write. However, a definition of simple reading and writing assumes uniformity among all participants and tools and does not account for transformations in language. Ong (1982) argues that the ability to encode information in new ways increases the possibilities of a language, can "restructure thought," and capture new meaning with the help of new communications methods. This restructuring of thought, in turn, opens the door for new, emergent forms of communication and language use that can suit specific needs and desires, as well as foster progress in societies. As advances in literacy are "absolutely necessary for the development of not only science but also of history, philosophy, explicative understanding of literature or of any art, and indeed for the explanation of language" (pp. 15), digital technologies will inevitably influence the nature of literacy by creating new opportunities for expression and meaning. This could in turn create greater capabilities for the public to understand civic information and become involved in their communities.

Before digital literacy emerged as a research focus of its own, scholars in the area of "new literacies" theorized that plural literacy skills exist. The understanding of plural literacies started to replace the more traditional definition of literacy, or the simple ability to read and write (Barton, 1994; Street, 1995; Kress, 2003; Cope & Kalantzis, 2000; Snyder, 2002). Plural literacies do not just represent the ability to interpret and create language in multiple formats, but also the mastery of the tools by which people communicate and the social contexts under which communication is used. As such, literary scholars frequently suggest that there is not a single overarching description of literacy skills across domains, as these skills are socially situated and contextual (Gee, 2008; Scribner & Cole, 1981; Street, 1995). Plural literacies are not just defined by the possession of discrete skills, but it also includes the mastery of the practices or processes of communication within a situational context (Lankshear &

Knobel, 2006). This notion of literacy includes both tangible, measurable skills (such as the ability to read and write) and other intangible skills (the ability to interpret communications based on social context or to think critically). As language itself is just as important as the media with which the language is encoded and decoded, this focus area considers mastery of both the tools for communication and the information the tools contain.

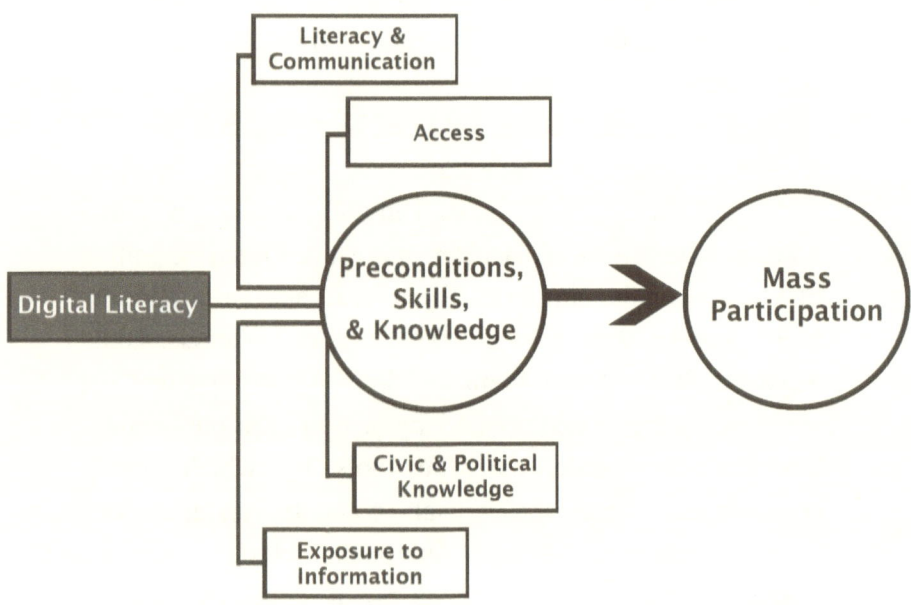

Figure 2.2
Relationship between Digital Literacy and Mass
Participation (including other antecedent resources)

2.5 – DOMAINS OF DIGITAL LITERACY

The literature on digital literacy largely theorizes the different types of skills that are required for a digitally literate person. As of writing this, few empirical studies have been presented in the literature on the observed presence of digital literacy and its influence on mass participation. I reviewed theories on digital literacy and defined several competency areas with which I can demonstrate the strength of various digital literacy skills. In this thesis, I identify six domains of digital literacy skills and knowledge that people can apply to their mass participation activities: computer skills, information skills, communication skills, publication skills, innovative thinking, and cultural and historical knowledge. As outlined in Table 2.2, these six domains encompass several discrete technology, information processing, and thinking skills that are necessary for the efficient operation of information technologies. Mastery in these six domains could give an individual an advantage with mass participation activities through the advanced capability for communication that digital literacy enables. These six domains, however, are closely related and many skills and knowledge areas are difficult to observe or categorize. Digital literacy theorists have accordingly developed research to explore and debate what digital literacy skills look like, under what conditions they emerge, and how certain categories of skills relate to other digital literacy skills.

Six Domains of Digital Literacy

1. *Computer Skills*

2. *Information Skills*

3. *Communication Skills*

4. *Publication Skills*

5. *Innovative Thinking*

6. *Cultural and Historical Knowledge*

Table 2.2
Six Domains of Digital Literacy

The first step toward using digital tools to retrieve and use information is acquiring the skills required to use the technology. Categorized as what I call *computer skills,* these abilities are often characterized by competency with computational basics, hardware, software, and networks (Jenkins, 2006a; International Technology Education Association, 2002; Trilling & Fadel, 2009). Basic information technology competency appears in virtually every study of digital literacy as it is the foundation upon which all other digital literacy skills are based. However, scholars note that a mastery of operating technology does not alone create the digitally literate person. Pearson and Young (2002) note that technical capability is only one part of the equation, stressing that more intangible "ways of thinking and acting" and other knowledge on the culture of technology and its risks and rewards is equally necessary (pp. 14-22). Other scholars agree with this necessity of multi-level competency past the actual technical skills (Lankshear & Knobel, 2008; Martin, 2010; Dede; 2010). Computer skills are only one dimension of digital literacy, albeit an important one. Despite my attempt in this thesis to create robust measures of computer skills, these skills differ as widely due the black-boxed nature of many computing systems. As such, it is likely that people can still participate at a fairly high level without deep knowledge of how the intricacies of information technologies and networks function down to the circuit level.

Scholars have theorized that digital literacy should also include the non-discrete skills of acquiring, synthesizing, and judging the quality of information. Digital literacy also includes what I call here *information skills*, or the ability to retrieve, analyze, and apply information from digital platforms. Because information has become increasingly difficult to divorce from the media and technologies that deliver it, scholars assert that it is essential to simultaneously know how to use digital tools as well as the information they contain (Bawden, 2001; Snavely & Cooper, 1997). Gilster (1997), who was the first to popularly use the term digital literacy, was careful to note this dual mastery of tools and information by saying digital literacy was just as much about "mastering ideas, and not keystrokes." In addition, with the onslaught of information available on the Internet, the ability to efficiently navigate the deluge of data is increasingly valuable in daily life (Rushkoff, 2010).

The need to communicate effectively over multiple media is an equally important domain of digital literacy. The domains of *communications skills* and *creative and publication skills* address the ability to read and write electronic texts and create compelling messages in the digital multimedia ecosystem.

Specifically, *communications skills* are those with which people send and receive electronic messages (competency with the means of communication), while *creative and publication skills* are those with which people create and distribute multimedia content to various audiences (competency with creating information). Media scholars highlight the different styles of information and messages that can be conveyed with multimedia tools. They have found that vast differences in interpretation and context exist between various combinations of visual, auditory, aesthetic, and interactive elements that can be employed in today's communications (Tyner, 1998; Hobbs, 1998; Buckingham, 2003; Wilde & Wilde, 1991). As media forms converge and in effect create newer forms of communication and expression (Jenkins, 2006b), the digitally literate person needs to know how to combine media in various ways to create different publications that maximize the strengths of each medium. It is within this realm that traditional literacy is most closely aligned: the ability to read and write in various multimedia contexts. As such, the ability to express oneself digitally is a valuable skill for mass participation as it empowers the public to have a more diverse voice that can maximize media elements to one's advantage.

In addition to technology and information skills that are essential for digital literacy, scholars suggest that those who build mental models to identify problems, hypothesize solutions, and value an experimental attitude in digital environments are generally more successful at tasks involving digital technologies (International Technology Eductaion Association, 2002; Jenkins, 2006a; Pearson & Young, 2006; North Central Regional Educational Laboratory & The Metiri Group, 2003). Skills that mirror those of the scientific and engineering community fall in the digital literacy domain that I call *innovative thinking*. As represented in the literature on both digital literacy and inquiry-based scientific literacy, innovative thinking skills include critical thinking, habits of iterative and experimental activity, and inventive or creative tendency with technology. Past research also suggests that skills in this domain enable flexibility in learning new technologies, likely due to the appreciation for iteration and progressive improvement of models (Jenkins, 2006a; American Association for the Advancement of Science, 1990)

The final domain of digital literacy that I examine common to the literature is that of *cultural and historical knowledge.* To prevent technology lock-in or unforeseen negative consequences, Americans need to know the basic technology issues and contexts that accompany the knowledge economy. This includes an understanding of the risks associated with any use of technology, the possibility of loss of information or mistranslation when using digital tools in various social contexts, and legal or social issues that affect technology use (Pearson & Young, 2002; Jenkins, 2006a; Trilling & Fadel, 2009). Privacy and the implications of an online persona is another key knowledge area, which includes items such as knowing how to manipulate the various Facebook and Twitter privacy controls and why they matter. Knowing privacy controls and their implications become especially important when technologies change their default access or interface, such as in the case of Facebook's recent transition to the Timeline format, which had dramatic social consequences for those who were less informed of Facebook's privacy controls. This category also includes an understanding of the programmed nature of technology, or that all technologies have been designed under certain parameters to serve a certain purpose. Rushkoff (2010) argues that technologies embody the values of their designers and that people should know these frameworks in order to meet their personal goals, not the goals of the designers. By admonishing his readers to learn to "program or be programmed," Rushkoff asserts that a broader knowledge of the underlying social constructs and learning the reasons under which technologies are designed is extremely valuable for the digitally literate person. This knowledge would give people the ability to use technologies in new ways and anticipate the effects they would have on various communities or on public participation.

2.6 – THEORETICAL FRAMEWORK AND HYPOTHESES

My goal for this thesis is to analyze how the possession of digital literacy skills influences mass participation in America. I accomplish this by conducting several hypothesis tests that place digital literacy as an antecedent skill for various mass participation activities. To avoid spurious results, I control for demographic factors and political identification, all of which likely influence a person's propensity for mass participation.

My primary argument in this thesis is that digital literacy is now an antecedent skill for mass participation. As such, I suggest that it should join the ranks of other required resources that citizens need for effective participation. Figure 2.3 illustrates the model under which I make these arguments. As demonstrated by the six small boxes on the left side of the model in Figure 2.3, six dimensions of digital literacy compose the complete digital literacy concept that I examine (which is indicated by large circle). I hypothesize that higher levels of digital literacy will predict higher levels of mass participation. This relationship is indicated by the large arrow in the center of the model. I also hypothesize that because of the increased digital media environment surrounding modern American politics, digital literacy is more relevant for political participation when compared to the three domains of traditional mass participation (social membership, civic, and political). In addition to this primary relationship, I assume that several independent control variables including socioeconomic status and political identification will influence this relationship (indicated by gray ovals). Using data from several digital literacy indicators provided by the 2012 Technology Use Survey, I illustrate the antecedent digital literacy skills that strongly lead to mass participation. In addition, my thesis seeks to establish baseline indicators that can be used to track digital literacy trends over time.

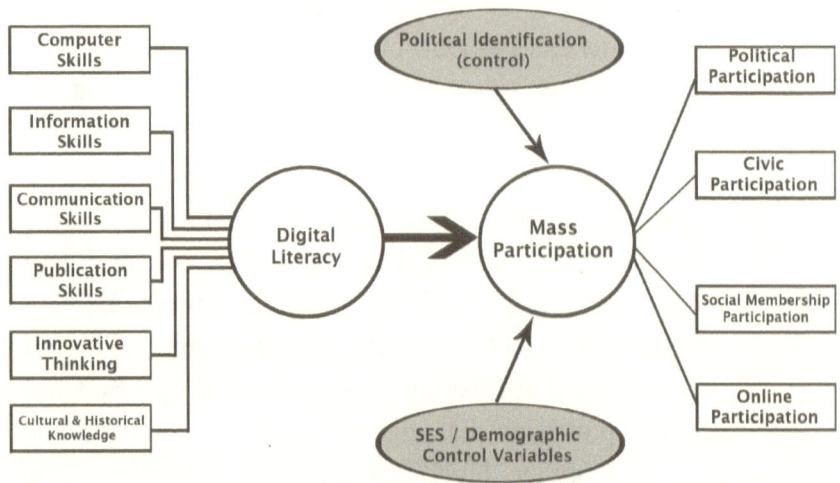

Figure 2.3
Thesis Theoretical Framework

2.6.1 – Research Questions

I ask the following primary research question to guide this study: **To what degree is digital literacy a predictor of mass participation?** In addition, as digital literacy has yet to be studied in-depth within the realm of participation, I ask the following questions to guide the construction of the measures used in this thesis: **What digital literacy skills are used in daily life? Are any digital literacy skills required for mass participation (i.e., are *antecedent* to participation)?**

2.6.2 – Hypotheses

To provide evidence for the relationships between digital literacy and mass participation, I test the following hypotheses in this thesis:

H_1: Knowledge of cultural and historical issues of technology is correlated the most with higher levels of mass participation when compared to the other five domains of digital literacy

H_2: Digital literacy skills that are used for creativity and content publication are correlated with higher levels mass participation when compared to computer, information, and communication skills

H_3: Digital literacy is the strongest predictor of traditional mass participation when compared to strength of political ideology and social demographics

H_4: Online participation is influenced the most by digital literacy skills when compared across the four domains of mass participation

H_5: Higher levels of digital literacy predict higher levels of political participation

CHAPTER 3 – METHODS

3.1 – METRIC DEVELOPMENT AND STUDY DESIGN

3.1.1 – Survey Design

To collect empirical data for this thesis, I created a nationally representative survey to compare levels of digital literacy to mass participation activities. Since much of the previous work in digital literacy to date has been theoretical, I required a set of baseline indicators with which I could test my hypotheses. As such, I created a series of survey indicators that correspond to the six digital literacy domains that I discussed in Chapter 2: computer skills, information skills, communication skills, publication skills, innovative thinking, and cultural and historical knowledge. These questions were informed by previous work that theorized and categorized digital literacy skills (e.g., National Research Council, 1999; Pearson & Young, 2002; North Central Regional Educational Laboratory & The Metiri Group, 2003; Jenkins, 2006a; Eshet-Alkalai, 2004; Hargittai, 2005; Martin, 2005, 2010). 59 separate indicators of skills and knowledge related to digital literacy were included on the survey. Because each domain was not uniformly prioritized among all the studies, I wanted to avoid leaving any key skill out of the measure and included indicators for all domains that I found consistently throughout the literature. I merged the six domains into an omnibus index in order to test my hypotheses. Survey respondents were asked to answer questions from a range of 1 (not at all skilled) to 5 (very skilled/expert) on each of the 59 indicators of skills and knowledge. Each of these indicators was informed by past theory on digital literacy, I operationalized them into discrete tasks that measure competence or knowledge with particular digital literacy activities. Each of the indicators that I used to measure digital literacy is detailed in Appendix I.

Similar to digital literacy, I developed survey questions to measure respondent levels of mass participation in four domains. The measures that I used expand upon the civic and political participation survey questions used by Putnam (2000) in his classic *Bowling Alone* study, which were specifically drawn from the methodology in the Roper Social and Political Trends Data study, 1973-1994 (Roper, 1994). I expanded these indicators in the Putnam/Roper survey from requiring a dichotomous response (e.g., "Did you participate in X activity?" Yes/no) to instead allowing respondents to indicate the level of their activity on a scale from 1 to 5. The numeric scores represented no activity in the last year (1) to frequent activity/served as a leader or organizer (5) on 48 mass participation activities within four domains. In addition to the questions that were applied directly from the Roper methodology (see Appendix III), I added multiple original questions that further gauge mass participation, particularly those that involve Internet and computer-mediated activity. This included a battery of questions that I developed that specifically discuss online-only social activities. Each of the indicators that I used to measure mass participation is detailed in Appendix II.

The complete survey is provided in Appendix IV. Respondents also answered 10 questions on their demographic and background information. In addition to the digital literacy and participation indicators, I also developed a variety of other original questions for this survey that gauged respondent attitudes and behaviors toward technology education, mass participation, and the value they gain from technology in their daily lives. However, many of these questions were not used directly in this thesis.

3.1.2 – The Digital Literacy Indexes and Operational Definitions

To measure the concept of digital literacy, I created the omnibus Digital Literacy Index (DLI). This index is composed of the 42 indicators of digital literacy collected in the 2012 Technology Use Survey mentioned in the section above. The index gives each respondent a DLI score that is proportionate to how they responded to the 42 indicators of digital literacy skill and knowledge. The DLI was found to be highly reliable (Cronbach's α: .910). As the DLI is an additive scale, missing values within any indicator could dramatically skew a respondent's score toward the low end of the scale. To mitigate this, the median value for a particular indicator in the sample replaced missing values before the DLI was constructed.

In addition to the DLI, I created six additional indexes that operationalize specific categories of skills and constitute the broader concept of digital literacy, which are outlined in Table 3.1. Similar to the DLI, each of these indicators was found to be highly reliable and I replaced any missing values in an indicator with the median value for that particular indicator. These indexes are used to further explore relationships between these more specific domains of digital literacy and mass participation. Details on the specific survey indicators that were used to construct these indexes are available in Appendix I.

	Total # of indicators	Cronbach's α
The *Computer Skills Index*, which is operationally represented by survey indicators that demonstrate skills with computer hardware, interface, and computer operating systems	12	.924
The *Information Skills Index*, which is operationally represented by survey indicators that demonstrate skills with retrieving, analyzing, and synthesizing information from networked computer and information technology devices	10	.892
The *Communication Skills Index,* which is operationally represented by survey indicators that demonstrate skills with sending and receiving information and content with other people across digital networks	12	.936

The *Creativity and Publication Skills Index*, which is operationally represented by survey indicators that demonstrate ability to create text, audio, video, and other multimedia projects or content and distribute that content to various audiences	11	.917
The *Innovative Thinking Index*, which is operationally represented by survey indicators that demonstrate the ability for critical thinking, iterative and experimental activity, and inventive or creative tendency with technology	5	.803
The *Cultural and Historical Knowledge Index*, which is operationally represented by survey indicators that demonstrate knowledge on the cultural risks and benefits of technology, current laws and social norms regarding technology, and how technology trends influence social action, and vice versa.	9	.930

Table 3.1

Operational Sub-Indexes: Domains of Digital Literacy
(see Appendix I for more details)

3.1.3 – The Mass Participation Indexes and Operational Definitions

I created the omnibus Traditional Participation Index to measure overall mass participation in community and political affairs. This index combines three types of

46

traditional mass participation: social membership participation, civic participation, and political participation. In this measure, I attempt to exclude emergent forms of social engagement that occur in an online-only space. This is done in order to capture the effects of digital literacy on the more traditional forms of mass participation and compare results to online forms of participation. In order to compare to emerging forms of online participation, I define traditional mass participation as mass participation activities that are not performed solely online, reflecting activities that existed before the development of the Internet. With the advent of the Internet, however, has come an unavoidable crossover of the online and offline participatory environments, and I assume a degree of intermingling is unavoidable between these categories.

The Traditional Participation Index (TPI) combines 34 indicators of participation in the three domains of traditional participation (social membership, civic, and political participation). These indicators were drawn from questions on the 2012 Technology Use Survey, with each indicator measuring the level of participation in a specific activity. The TPI operationalizes these indicators of participation onto a numeric scale, with a higher value indicating a higher level of participation in a particular activity. The TPI was found to be highly reliable (Cronbach's α: .927) when all 34 indicators were combined. Removing any indicator from the index would not cause a significantly higher or lower reliability coefficient.

I also created three separate indexes for the three types of mass participation that compose the TPI: The Social

Membership Participation Index, the Civic Participation Index, and the Political Participation Index. These three indexes measure the constituent parts of the TPI and allow for greater specification of the influence that digital literacy has on the various forms of participation. Details on these three indexes are found in Table 3.2. For each indicator in the TPI and its three constituent sub-indexes, missing values were replaced with the median score for a particular indicator in order to mitigate skewness toward a score of zero if a particular case exhibits missing values.

Drawing from theory that suggests that new forms of mass participation might be moving to online-only spaces, I also created the Online Participation Index, which measures the degree that people participated in online-only social activities. Defined, online participation is voluntary activity in which an individual takes part in or shares in activities for personal growth and common interests, but does so solely over the Internet and other networked electronic communications. This includes activities such as meeting new people online, connecting with friends online, and sharing common interests with others online. The Online Participation Index is measured with 9 separate indicators from the survey that fall within this definition. It is possible that the Online Participation Index reliability coefficient might be lower the other three sub-domains because of the novelty of this measure: these indicators have not yet been used in a study of mass participation and require further analysis that comes with additional study.

Methods

	Total # of indicators	Cronbach's α
The *Social Membership Participation Index*, which is operationally represented by survey indicators that depict in-person, voluntary activity in which an individual takes part in or shares in activities for personal growth and common interests	11	.830
The *Civic Participation Index*, which is operationally represented by survey indicators that depict organized voluntary activity either alone or with others in which a person's work is focused on problem solving or helping others	9	.838
The *Online Participation Index,* which is operationally represented by survey indicators that depict voluntary activity in which an individual takes part in or shares in activities for personal growth and common interests, but does so solely over the Internet and other networked electronic communications and does not overtly attempt to discuss or influence political action	8	.797

The *Political Participation Index,* which is operationally represented by survey indicators that depict activity either alone or with others in which a person's activity is related to influencing government or elected official action, either directly or indirectly	14	.897

Table 3.2

Operational Sub-Indexes: Domains of Participation
(see Appendix II for more details)

Online participation is similar to the social membership participation domain, with the difference being that the Online Participation Index only measures activities that take place solely on the Internet or via other networked devices. As I defined here, an individual can participate online and subsequently meet those he/she meets outside of the online space, but at that point, it would cease to be online participation and become social membership participation.

Details on the specific survey questions that were used to construct these indexes and operationalize these concepts are available in Appendix II.

3.2 – DATA COLLECTION: THE 2012 TECHNOLOGY USE SURVEY

I used results from the 2012 Technology Use Survey as my primary data source. The survey collected information on respondent digital literacy skills as well as their mass participation behaviors and attitudes.

The survey was administered over the Internet by using Mechanical Turk by Amazon.com (http://www.mturk.com), a service that enables "requesters" to pay "responders" to complete small tasks, including scientific surveys. Respondents were recruited through the service and answered survey questions inside of a web browser by clicking responses appropriate to their choice. Respondents were not connected to the investigator in any way and were recruited by Mechanical Turk after viewing a welcome message by the investigator.

To qualify for the survey, respondents were required to be a registered member of the Mechanical Turk service, be a United States resident, and be over 18 years old. In addition, respondents were required to have an approval rating of at least 95% with past work performed on the Mechanical Turk service, a control measure kept by the Mechanical Turk service to encourage quality work among respondents. Respondents were compensated with a nominal fee for their involvement upon completing the entire survey, paid directly by Mechanical Turk to the respondent.

The survey was launched on February 28, 2012 and closed on March 15, 2012. The survey provided a random sample size of 1180 valid responses.

3.3 – ANALYSIS METHODS

I employed the Digital Literacy Index, Traditional Participation Index, and Online Participation Index mentioned in the survey construction methodology section to examine the influence of digital literacy as an antecedent skill for mass participation. I offer a series of descriptive statistics from the survey to provide a snapshot into the current state of digital literacy and participation in its various forms in the United States. In addition to the descriptive analysis, I tested five hypotheses by using a series of OLS regression and correlation models in which I demonstrated the strength by which digital literacy and its sub-domains of competency influence the differing types of participation in the United States today. I controlled for demographic and political identification factors to increase the specification of the relationship between digital literacy and participation. These control variables include gender, age, education level, employment status, household income, party identification, and strength of political ideology.

3.3.1 – Adjusted Summary Scales for Descriptive Means Comparison

For the descriptive comparison between domains of digital literacy and mass participation, I created *adjusted summary scales*. These summary scales, which are all measured with values of 1 to 5, were derived from the original indexes mentioned in sections 3.1.2 and 3.1.3. This transformation was necessary in order to compare the six digital literacy domain indexes, as each index created in section 3.1.2 has a different range of values. This also applies to the four indexes of participation created in section 3.1.3. Summary measure indexes are only used for comparative purposes in the descriptive analysis and are not used to test hypotheses in this thesis. To make these adjustments, each summary scale was assigned a value according to a two-step process. First, I calculated the mean score for each indicator that appeared in an index. Second, since each indicator was scored on the same scale of 1 to 5, I calculated the mean score of all indicators appearing within an index and assigned this result as the summary scale value (represented as *SumScl*). Figure 3.1 illustrates the equation by which the summary scales were assigned values of *SumScl*, with *n* equal to the total number of indicators appearing in each index. A total of 7 digital literacy summary scales (1 omnibus scale and 6 sub-domains) and 5 participation summary scales were created for this comparison (1 ombibus scale and 4 sub-domain scales).

$$SumScl = \frac{\sum_{i=1}^{n} \bar{x}_i}{n}$$

Figure 3.1
Summary Scale Value Equation, *SumScl*
(used for each summary scale)

For digital literacy, each summary scale was adjusted to represent a range of low digital literacy (score of 1) to high digital literacy (score of 5). For the measure of mass participation and its four domains, each summary scale was adjusted to represent a range of low participation (score of 1) to high participation (score of 5). I discussed the mean scores of the seven summary digital literacy scales (adjusted summaries of the full index and six constituent indexes) and illustrated observed differences between domains of digital literacy skills. Similarly, I reviewed the scores of the five summary participation scales (the adjusted summary traditional participation scale and the four sub-domains of participation) and show the observed differences between types of participation accordingly.

3.3.2 – Descriptive Analysis and Demographic Comparisons

I ran a series of frequencies distributions and difference of means tests to provide descriptive analyses of public levels of digital literacy and mass participation in their various forms. These measures are cross-compared with common social demographics such as gender, age, education, and income. This section highlights the various differences in both digital literacy and mass participation among social demographic groups in the United States.

To observe differences between the six domains of digital literacy as well as the four domains of participation, I compared the means of the several summary scale measures created in Section 3.1. To illustrate differences of summary scale scores between common demographic groups within the public, I used ANOVA and independent samples t-test analyses to determine differences in mean scores of the summary measures based on group membership. In this section, I highlighted differences in the summary scale scores for digital literacy and mass participation between gender, education level, and age.

3.3.3 – Hypothesis Testing and Analysis

To test the hypotheses in this thesis, I employed a series of ordinary least-squares regressions and Pearson's R correlations to determine the strength and direction of the influence of digital literacy on the various domains of mass participation. The concepts of digital literacy and mass participation are analyzed as measured by the omnibus Digital Literacy Index, the omnibus Traditional Participation Index, and the constituent participation domain indexes discussed in Section 3.1.3. For each analysis, one of the participation indexes serves as the dependent variable in the equation.

For the first analysis, I compared each domain of digital literacy to the Traditional Participation Index using bivariate Pearson's R analyses to assess the strength of each of the six individual sub-categories of digital literacy on mass participation. By using the Pearson's R coefficients, I am able to see the strength of correlation between a particular digital literacy domain and levels of traditional mass participation. Using this method, I compare the Pearson's R coefficients to see which digital literacy domain influences mass participation in the strongest manner. Each of the six domains of digital literacy is highly correlated with each other (i.e., each bivariate comparison demonstrating over a .600 Pearson's

R coefficient). This method allows me to demonstrate the strength of digital literacy domains while avoiding methodological violations with OLS regression models.

In the second analysis, I test the influence of digital literacy on the omnibus Traditional Participation Index using an OLS regression model that includes demographic and political identification control variables. In the final analysis, I test the influence of digital literacy on the individual participation indexes using a series of OLS regressions, in which the beta coefficients for each variable are compared across domains. For each analysis, the omnibus Digital Literacy Index serves as an independent variable to predict levels of participation alongside a series of control variables. These controls include age, gender, education level, employment status, household income, party identification, and strength of political ideology.

CHAPTER 4 – DESCRIPTIVE DIFFERENCES IN DIGITAL LITERACY AND MASS PARTICIPATION

In this chapter, I provide a snapshot of the current levels of the digital literacy skills of Americans and illustrate how often Americans engage in mass participation activities. Using data from the 2012 Technology Use Survey, I highlight differences in digital literacy skills and mass participation within two key demographics: gender and age. These analyses are drawn from the adjusted summary scales of each of the six domains of digital literacy and four domains of mass participation (mentioned in greater detail in section 3.1.4). Differences of means between groups are analyzed with independent samples t-tests and one-way ANOVA tests.

The descriptive statistics in this chapter show that younger people are better skilled with digital tools, males have a slight advantage in levels of digital literacy, and other demographics such as education level do not significantly indicate differences in digital literacy. These findings illustrate some of the current issues facing digital literacy acquisition and education in the United States. Primarily, as digital literacy has become an antecedent skill set for mass participation activities, these findings would indicate that groups such as older adults and females would be more disadvantaged when it comes to participatory activities. Mastery of digital literacy skills will be essential to effect social change or to even join a social group as information technologies are increasingly used in the participatory environment. As more information-heavy jobs become the norm in the 21st Century knowledge economy, it will also be increasingly important for people of all ages and education levels to have a high level of digital literacy.

I also illustrate how the public was engaged in mass participation activities in 2011-2012 using observed adjusted mean scores within participation domains. To explore the degree to which online participation patterns compare to more traditional forms of mass participation, I sort the four domains of participation into two categories: traditional participation (consisting of social membership, civic, and political participation) and online participation (consisting only of the online measure). By comparing the mean summary values for the four mass participation domain summary scales, I found that the public engaged in more social online participation activities than those of the other three more traditional forms of mass participation. This could be indicative of a shift in participation due to the relative ease of online communication in comparison more traditional forms of mass participation, especially those that require in-person presence.

4.1 – DIGITAL LITERACY IN THE UNITED STATES

4.1.1 – Computer and Information Skills Are High, But People Have Fewer Creative Skills

By comparing the mean scores of the six summary scales of digital literacy, I found that people generally scored high (4 out of 5) with mastery of discrete computer skills (such as using the Internet or setting up a computer; mean score 4.05), communication skills (such as sending an email or using instant messaging; mean score 4.23), and information skills (such as knowing the original authorship of a document; mean score 4.10). However, scores are much lower for creative and expressive skills, as demonstrated by the publication skills (such as creating word documents or creating an audio clip; mean score 3.29) and innovative thinking domains (such trying something many times to get it right or a habit of customization with technology; mean score 3.22). Historical and cultural knowledge was the lowest observed measure of digital literacy among the public (mean score 2.60). Figure 4.1 illustrates the differences in mean scores for each of the six domains of digital literacy.

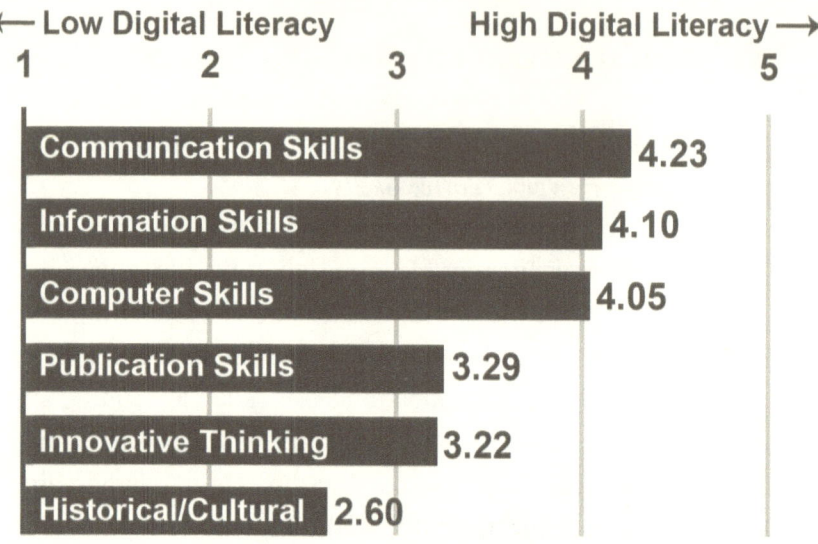

Figure 4.1

Summary Scale Mean Scores for Digital Literacy Domains
(based on summary scale mean scores; $n = 1180$)

Lower digital literacy scores in the creative/innovative domains could be due to the higher degree of effort required to publish documents and digital texts. In a busy work and life environment, it takes more time to acquire the skills for digital publication and expression. This lower level could also be indicative of the values surrounding digital technologies and might represent less of an emphasis or value among the public on the ability to create digital items or express oneself using digital media. Publication and innovative thinking skills are more representative of the ability to solve problems and to "think outside the box," whereas computer, information, and communication skills generally represent tasks that can be described in a step-by-step process. These discrete skills can be replicated in the same way each time, making them easier to accomplish. Digital literacy researchers, however, stress the importance of these non-discrete problem solving, creative, and iterative thinking skills when working with information technologies, indicating that it leads to a greater level of success in whatever task in which they use these digital technologies (Gilster, 1997; Pearson & Young, 2002; Lankshear & Knobel, 2008). These data show that while people have higher levels of the discrete skills in operating computers, which is possibly due to their unavoidable ubiquity in the workplace and daily life, the acquisition of digital creativity and innovative thinking skills appears to be a lower priority for people.

Also interesting is the lower score in the historical and cultural knowledge digital literacy domain in comparison to the other domains. This domain represents knowledge of current issues facing technology, such as privacy, online identity, intellectual property law, and the benefits and challenges of adopting technologies for certain tasks. It appears that the public shows a lower level of knowledge about such issues than other discrete computer skills when scored on the same scale. As these fundamental issues can influence the use of information technology in society, the implications of not having stronger knowledge of these issues could be disadvantageous for mass participation activities. Future study in this area would be helpful to the field in understanding the influence of these cultural technology issues on social life and mass participation.

4.1.2 – Men Have Higher Levels of Digital Literacy

Figure 4.2 illustrates the difference in digital literacy skills (as measured by the omnibus adjusted summary scale) separated by gender. Using an independent samples t-test, the difference in mean scores between men and women was statistically significant at the $p < .000$ level.

While it is beyond the scope of this thesis to speculate the reasons for differences between genders, it appears that males have a slight advantage in digital literacy skills. However, this gap is not extremely wide, and could potentially close as information technology skills become more prioritized in the economy and as educational initiatives encourage people to enter careers that require higher levels of digital literacy, such as science, technology, engineering, and mathematics (STEM) career fields.

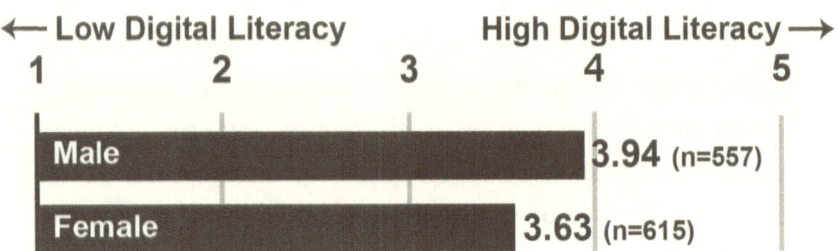

Figure 4.2
Digital Literacy by Gender
(based on summary scale mean score; total *n* = 1180)

4.1.3 – Young People Have Higher Levels of Digital Literacy

Young people have been popularly known as the "net generation" or as "digital natives" and are frequently regarded to have higher levels of digital literacy than older age cohorts. The data in this thesis show no exception to this trend. Differences between mean scores among age groups reveals a downward directional trend in digital literacy mean scores as age increases. Figure 4.3 highlights this observation, with younger people exhibiting higher mean scores of digital literacy than those of older cohorts.

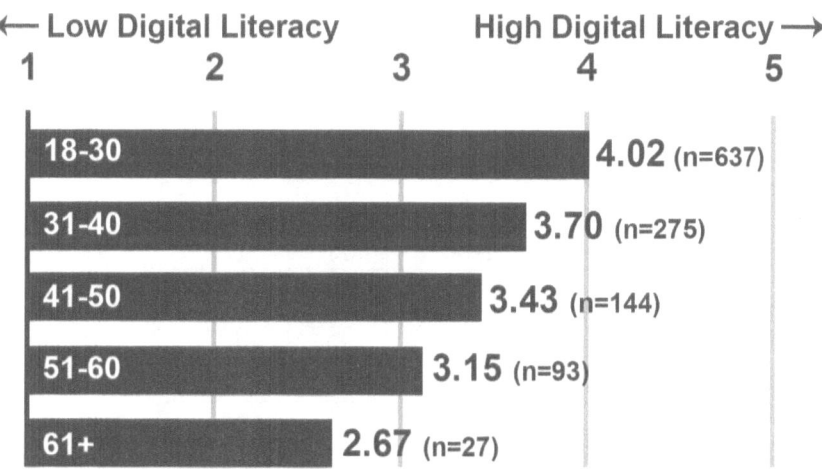

Figure 4.3
Digital Literacy by Age
(based on summary scale mean score; total $n = 1180$)

To test for significant differences between mean digital literacy scores by age group, I ran a one-way between-subjects ANOVA test (F = 39.04; p < .001) on digital literacy skills grouped by an age factor. Post hoc comparisons using the Tamhane's T-2 test, which indicate a true difference of means if the comparison is statistically significant, showed that the mean score the 18-30 age group was significantly different than all other age groups (see Table 4.1 for post-hoc results). In fact, all age groups are significantly different from one another (at p < .05 or greater) when comparing mean scores between groups with the exception of three comparisons: 31-40 to 41-50, 41-50 to 51-60, and 51-60 to over 61.

Comparison	Sig.	Std. Error
18-30 *to* 31-40	.000	.062
18-30 *to* 41-50	.000	.098
18-30 *to* 51-60	.000	.128
18-30 *to* 61+	.000	.226
31-40 *to* 41-50	.067	.099
31-40 *to* 51-60	.000	.128
31-40 *to* 61+	.001	.226
41-50 *to* 51-60	.411	.143
41-50 *to* 61+	.026	.235
51-60 *to* 61+	.454	.249

Table 4.1
Digital Literacy Differences of Means between Age Groups
(One-way ANOVA post-hoc test; Tamhane's T-2)
Significant comparisons at p < 0.05 are shaded in gray

Regardless of the lack of significant differences between older age groups, these results show that younger people have higher levels of digital literacy. As digital literacy is an antecedent skill for mass participation, these data indicate that young people have an advantage in their ability to participate.

4.1.4 – Other Demographic Differences

Gender and age provide two good examples of digital literacy division among demographic groups. When testing other demographics, however, group differences are either not statistically significant. This holds true for education, employment level, and city size (urban/suburban/rural).

4.2 – MASS PARTICIPATION IN THE UNITED STATES, 2011-2012

4.2.1 – People Choose Online Participation over Other Domains of Mass Participation

This thesis measures four different domains of mass participation and how they are influenced by digital literacy skills. Using the adjusted summary scales for these four domains, I compared levels of observed participation across domains, as illustrated in Figure 4.4. While participation is relatively low in all four domains (scoring between 1 and 2 on a 1-5 scale), online participation appears to be much higher than the other three domains of participation.

Figure 4.4

Mass Participation Domain Summary Index Mean Scores
(based on summary scale mean scores; $n = 1180$)

Based on the observed mean scores, online participation is almost half-point higher in frequency than the other three domains, which, on a 1-5 scale, indicates a large degree of variation. Since the three domains of social membership, civic, and political participation represent more traditional forms of mass participation, I assert that online participation has become a new favorite domain of participation among the public for socialization and meeting others. I also argue that this may not indicate trouble for the other three domains of participation. Online participation could encourage participants to engage in other forms of participation with whom they meet and interact online. In addition, people could learn about activities in other participation domains online.

I want to note, however, that these data indicate that *some activity* is present in all domains, even though each domain appears to be scored low. If the public engaged in no activity, the mean scores would be much closer to 1.0 than they appear. No participation within a domain would require respondents to answer 1, which indicates "never" on the survey (See Appendixes II and IV for more details on survey question scoring. While this is not a *lot* of activity, it certainly suggests that people have been at least somewhat active during the last year since higher scores (i.e., 3 or 4) on this index would correspond to scoring high on *all* indicators. Scoring very high on this scale would be close to impossible, as a high score corresponds to people participating frequently in *every* activity contained within these scales (each scale ranging from 9 to 14 separate activities). As such, I infer that people are participating in all domains, but not nearly to the degree they are participating in the online domain, which is much higher.

With daily life being busy and demanding for many Americans, it is understandable that mass participation levels are not extremely high. The cultures of work and home do not demand a robust social life or constant involvement in philanthropic or political service activities. Schudson (1999) argues that this is actually normal, with people today delegating much of their political and social affairs to others that can be responsible for them on a daily basis. This has allowed for specialists in the civic and political participation realm, such as politicians, political aides, and bureaucrats, to focus on activities of governance and social change. This isn't to say that the public is inattentive, however. Schudson asserts that the "monitorial citizen" is now present, or the citizen that pays attention to current affairs and will become active in civic or political affairs only after their participation becomes necessary, such as when situations become dire and an individual is spurred to volunteerism or political activity for a particular issue that they care about. In the mean time, people will instead delegate these civic and political tasks to specialists, allowing the non-specialists to live and work without too much mass participation.

4.3 – DISCUSSION OF DESCRIPTIVE STATISTICS

As demonstrated in the next chapter, I find that digital literacy is an antecedent skill for mass participation. The breakdown of observed levels of digital literacy and participation by demographic in this chapter illustrate some of the challenges associated with mass participation in a digital age: a person needs proper digital skills in order to participate. Gaps in levels of digital literacy among demographic groups show a digital literacy advantage for some, but also provide a blueprint for fixing this digital literacy divide. The data show that younger people are highly advantaged when it comes to digital literacy skills. Men also have a slight digital advantage. These groups will likely continue to influence civic and political affairs in greater ways compared to their counterparts as they enjoy higher levels of digital literacy skills. Efforts to mitigate these differences, such as technology education initiatives and technology training targeted to specific demographics could help further develop these digital literacy skills to the point they become constant among demographic groups.

While digital literacy is not the only antecedent precondition for mass participation, it can certainly help someone participate when they feel compelled to do so.

Traditional participation infrastructure, antecedent skills, and social dynamics concerning political or social influence still likely determine social change and politics to a great degree. However, with the increasing integration of digital tools into the participatory environment, traditional influence hierarchies might be renegotiated as time goes on. Regardless, those with digital literacy skills will likely be more influential in communicating their needs and interests as well as connecting with others.

The issue remains, however, that people with digital literacy skills are better equipped for mass participation, and that the data from the comparisons in this chapter show varying levels of skills among the digital literacy domains. This is especially true regarding the dearth of creative publication and skills that was observed. As the publication skills domain has a high influence on mass participation activities, I make the argument that those with these more intangible, creative skills will enjoy a higher degree of success when attempting civic or political change. However, since these skills appear less frequently than discrete, technical computer and information skills, there is a need for more education and empowerment in this area. Positive effects provided by digital literacy could even carry over to a person's career or daily life, although this is an area for future study.

CHAPTER 5 – DATA ANALYSIS: THE INFLUENCE OF DIGITAL LITERACY ON MASS PARTICIPATION

Antecedents of effective mass participation include political and civic knowledge, political predisposition and personal background, media and information exposure, and access to technology, resources, or influence. The combination of these resources influences a person's predisposition to become involved in mass participation activities. My central argument in this thesis is that digital literacy is now an antecedent skill that empowers mass participation. To provide support for this argument, I analyze how digital literacy skills predict mass participation in its various domains using statistical analysis, with mass participation as the dependent variable.

In this thesis, I define digital literacy as the ability to efficiently use electronic, networked tools to find, evaluate, create, distribute, and synthesize electronically mediated information. I measure digital literacy in six domains: computer skills, information skills, communication skills, creative and publication skills, innovative thinking, and cultural and historical knowledge. Mass participation any active behavior in which individuals join, organize, persuade, help others, and share for the purposes of personal growth, service, or social or governmental change. I categorize mass participation in four domains: social membership, civic, political, and online participation. In addition, I use the omnibus Traditional Participation Index, which combines the three domains of social membership, civic, and political participation in order to provide an indicator of activity that is not conducted solely online.

This chapter is divided into three analysis sections. I test five hypotheses that examine the strength of digital literacy as an antecedent skill for participation and explain the findings. In the process of this analysis, I control for demographic and political identification variables that better specify these relationships. The hypothesis tests work together to provide a three-sided view of the relationship between digital literacy and mass participation. For the first analysis, I examine the degree to which each of the six domains of digital literacy is correlated with mass participation. I do this by using bivariate Pearson's R correlations and comparing the coefficients of each domain with each other. The second analysis examines the influence of digital literacy on the omnibus Traditional Participation Index, which serves to measure total level of mass participation. Using an ordinary least-squares (OLS) regression model, I analyze the predictive strength of digital literacy on mass participation. In third analysis, I use four OLS regression models simultaneously to study the predictive power of digital literacy on *each* individual domain of mass participation, with some interesting results.

5.1 – CULTURAL/HISTORICAL KNOWLEDGE AND CREATIVE PUBLISHING DIGITAL LITERACY SKILLS HAVE THE MOST INFLUENCE ON MASS PARTICIPATION

In this analysis, I look at the influence of each of the six domains of digital literacy on participation using the Traditional Participation Index. The strength of each domain of digital literacy is determined using bivariate Pearson's R correlation coefficients. I test the two following hypotheses in this analysis section:

H_1: Knowledge of cultural and historical issues of technology is correlated the most with higher levels of mass participation when compared to the other five domains of digital literacy.

H_2: Digital literacy skills that are used for creativity and content publication are correlated with higher levels mass participation when compared to computer, information, and communication skills

Table 5.1 illustrates the individual bivariate Pearson's R correlations for this analysis. I determine the individual digital literacy domains and how they are correlated with traditional and online participation, with a higher Pearson's R coefficient indicating a stronger relationship. In the analysis in Table 5.1, traditional participation is measured using the omnibus Traditional Participation Index, which includes social membership, civic, and political participation simultaneously. Online participation is measured using the omnibus Online Participation Index. Due to the high level of correlation between the digital literacy independent variables (Pearson's R over .600 for every comparison), I am unable to enter these domains individually into a conventional OLS regression model.

For this model, I controlled for strength of political ideology as a folded concept. In other words, I was not interested in whether someone was conservative or liberal, but instead whether they had strong ideological leanings or not. The ideology strength variable was coded as 1 for low level of ideological leaning, 2 for people who identify either as conservative or liberal, and 3 for people who identify as very conservative or very liberal. Drawing from past theory in political participation, I anticipate that a person's strength of political ideology will draw them toward mass participation. In the "other controls" section, I included demographic variables of age and education as well.

	Traditional	*Online*
Computer Skills	.112**	.260**
Information Skills	.164**	.315**
Communication Skills	.116**	.285**
Publication Skills	.243**	.380**
Innovative Thinking Skills	.099**	.288**
Historical/Cultural Knowledge	.290**	.398**
Strength of Ideology	.097**	.036
Age	-.059*	-.182**
Education Level	.061*	-.070*

Values in Pearson's R Coefficients. n = 1180

*, ** indicates significance at the 95% and 99% level, respectively

Table 5.1

Pearson's R Coefficients: Digital Literacy Domains on Mass Participation [Traditional Participation Index includes social membership, civic, and political participation]

Findings and Hypothesis Tests

Each of the correlations between digital literacy and participation domains was statistically significant. In all categories, digital literacy was more highly correlated with online participation than traditional participation. Historical and cultural knowledge represents the domain of digital literacy with the highest influence on both traditional and online participation (Pearson's R: .290 traditional; .398 online). This is followed closely by creative and publication skills (.243 traditional; .380 online). Computer skills (.112 traditional; .260 online), information skills (.112 traditional; .260 online), communication skills (.112 traditional; .260 online), and innovative thinking skills (.112 traditional; .260 online) all show a significant correlation to both traditional and online participation, but to a weaker degree than the other domains. The strength of ideology variable is only slightly related to mass participation in this model (.097 traditional; not significant for online participation). Since this model is not fully political in nature, ideology strength plays less of a role. The other control variables are significantly correlated and display significant, but generally weaker, relationships.

To test the Hypothesis 1, I compare the Pearson's R coefficients among the digital literacy domains. I hypothesize people with higher amounts of knowledge of the issues facing society related to technology will be more inclined to participate. This hypothesis is confirmed, as cultural and historical knowledge has the highest Pearson's R coefficients among the six digital literacy domains.

I also expect that creative and publication skills will be highly correlated with participation, more so than computer, information, and communication skills. To test Hypothesis 2, I examine the Pearson's R coefficients for these four domains. The data show that people with the advanced capability to express oneself, to share ideas with multimedia, and to create content that can be persuasive and engaging will be more inclined to participate, especially online. I can confirm this hypothesis.

These two hypotheses support the argument that the six domains of digital literacy are present in higher levels of participation activities. This is particularly true of the skills that are more creative (publication) and provide a greater context of the use of technology in society (social and historical knowledge). Although showing lower levels of relationship to participation, the domains with lower scores (computer, information, communication) provide necessary skills for higher-order publication and content-sharing skills. Additional studies that better specify this relationship between digital literacy domains could be useful for the social sciences in determining the effects of digital literacy on various social institutions and activities.

5.2 – DIGITAL LITERACY IS THE STRONGEST PREDICTOR OF HIGHER LEVELS OF TRADITIONAL MASS PARTICIPATION THAN DEMOGRAPHIC CONTROL VARIABLES

In this section, I run an OLS regression model to demonstrate how digital literacy influences participation. I chose to combine the six domains of digital literacy into a single, omnibus variable for this analysis as all of the six digital literacy domains are highly correlated and work together in many ways. By combining the domains, I attempt to capture as much of the interplay between skills as possible. Also, by testing digital literacy as a single variable, I want to test current digital literacy theory that suggests each of these domains is used in tandem as a single concept for many social activities.

For this analysis, omnibus Traditional Participation Index is the dependent variable. This measure represent a person's whole level of mass participation three domains: social membership, civic, political. To analyze the strength between variables as predictors of mass participation, I compare the beta coefficients (β) and their statistical significance. Table 5.2 illustrates the results from this regression equation. I use the regression beta coefficients to test the following hypothesis in this section:

H₃: Digital literacy is the strongest predictor of traditional mass participation when compared to strength of political ideology and social demographics

Independent Variable	β-coefficient
Digital Literacy Skills	.209**
(Omnibus)	(.018)
Age	-.002
	(.069)
Education	.062*
	(.389)
Household Income	.024
	(.491)
Gender	-.062*
	(1.490)
Strength of Ideology	.081**
	(1.047)
Identify Republican	.045
	(1.963)
Identify Democrat	.075*
	(1.688)
Employed Full-Time	-.030
	(1.729)
Employed Part-Time	.051
	(2.196)
Not employed – Looking for Work	-.066*
	(2.540)

Total R^2: .067**; $n = 1180$. Standard errors are reported in parentheses.

*, **, indicates significance at the 95% and 99% level, respectively

Table 5.2
Regression Results of Digital Literacy on Traditional Participation

Findings and Hypothesis Test

As indicated by the highest beta coefficient in Table 5.2, digital literacy is the strongest significant predictor of traditional participation when compared to demographic control variables. As such, I can support Hypothesis 3. This finding indicates that even in the presence of other variables that could predict someone's level of mass participation, digital literacy is an antecedent precondition that strongly predicts participation. As a person's digital literacy skills increase, so does the level of their mass participation.

This model also shows that males actually participate more than females, as indicated by a negative coefficient that is statistically significant. Also, the education variable is statistically significant, indicating that those of higher education level participate more than those of lower levels. The strength of a person's political ideology also was a significant predictor, showing that those who are highly ideological (i.e., *very* conservative or *very* liberal) will participate more than those who are neutral or independent. This is expected as ideologues generally participate more in community and public affairs. All independent variables showed low levels of correlation with each other, if any (Pearson's R < .200).

It is also of note to consider the other predictors of participation in this model. Age and household income are not significant in this model. While money is certainly a resource that assists in participation, it appears that income or other financial resources do not play a strong role in mass participation. Regarding the age variable, people of all age groups might be participating equally, as the variable is not a significant predictor of participation.

5.3 – DIGITAL LITERACY INFLUENCES ONLINE PARTICIPATION THE MOST AND DOES NOT INFLUENCE CIVIC PARTICIPATION

The final analysis that I perform takes a closer look at the influence of digital literacy on each individual domain of mass participation. To accomplish this, each domain of mass participation (social membership, civic, political, and online) serves as dependent variable in four separate OLS regression models. Included with the omnibus digital literacy index are political identity indicators including strength of political ideology and party identification. Also included are several demographic control variables, including age, education, household income, gender. These regression models use the same folded ideology variable as the one explained in Section 5.1. The results of the regression analysis are illustrated in Table 5.3. This analysis formally tests Hypotheses 4 and 5 to specify the relationship that digital literacy has on the various domains of participation.

H_4: Online participation is influenced the most by digital literacy skills when compared across the four domains of mass participation

H_5: Higher levels of digital literacy predict higher levels of political participation

Data Analysis

Independent Variable	Social Membership	Civic	Political	Online
Digital Literacy Skills	.123** (.005)	.043 (.004)	.130** (.006)	.353** (.004)
Age	-.118** (.019)	.022 (.017)	.058 (.024)	-.044 (.016)
Education	.120** (.106)	.043 (.094)	.034 (.034)	-.027 (.091)
Household Income	.036 (.134)	.059 (.118)	.030 (.233)	-.059* (.116)
Gender	-.082** (.407)	.051 (.359)	-.081* (.512)	-.073** (.351)
Strength of Ideology	-.040 (.286)	-.022 (.253)	.178** (.360)	.039 (.246)
Identify Republican	.070* (.536)	.100** (.474)	.005 (.675)	-.025 (.462)
Identify Democrat	.050 (.461)	.051 (.407)	.091** (.580)	.038 (.397)
Employed Full-Time	-.045 (.472)	.017 (.417)	-.015 (.594)	-.036 (.407)
Employed Part-Time	.057* (.600)	.079 (.530)	.021 (.755)	.027 (.517)

(con't on next page)

Not employed – Looking for Work	-.094** (.694)	-.053 (.613)	-.053* (0.873)	-.022 (.598)
R^2	.069**	.022**	.065**	.158**

$n = 1180$. Values in β-coefficients. Standard errors are reported in parentheses.

*, ** indicates significance at the 95% and 99% level, respectively

Table 5.3

(con't from page 81)

Regression Comparisons of Digital Literacy on Mass
Participation Domains

Findings and Hypothesis Tests

Digital literacy is a strong, significant predictor of online participation (β = .353). Given this observation, I can support Hypothesis 4. This is to be expected due to the inherently technical nature of the media used in online communication. Interesting, however, is the presence of only two other significant predictors in online participation, which are both negative in direction: household income and gender. Those with lower incomes participate online more, and men participate online more than women.

As demonstrated by the beta coefficients for each regression model in Table 5.3, digital literacy is a strongly significant predictor of participation in the social membership and political domains as well. However, digital literacy is not a significant predictor in the domain of civic participation, and, as such, serves no antecedent capacity for civic participation. In testing the hypothesis, digital literacy predicts political participation domain to a high degree compared to other predictors ($\beta = .130$). Digital literacy predicts political participation to a greater degree than in the other two traditional participation domains (Social membership $\beta = .123$; Civic participation $\beta = .043$/not significant). As digital literacy is a significant predictor of political participation, I can support Hypothesis 5.

Digital literacy is not the strongest predictor within the four domains of participation. For example, social membership participation appears to be influenced by three predictors almost equally: digital literacy, age, and education, with each having similar beta coefficients. While sharing similar strength with these predictors, digital literacy still empowers social membership participation. In a second example, digital literacy predicts political participation less than the strength of a person's ideology. This is to be expected as a person's ideology and political beliefs have been demonstrated to be a powerful indicator of a person's political involvement. Digital literacy still predicts higher levels of political participation, indicating its strength as an antecedent skill.

CHAPTER 6 – DISCUSSION OF FINDINGS

The three analyses in Chapter 5 work together to illustrate this thesis' key finding: digital literacy is an antecedent skill to most forms of mass participation. Those who have digital literacy skills are more empowered to participate. In effect, digital literacy skills have become a new set of civic skills that enable people to participate more effectively in their communities and in political matters. I found that while digital literacy is not as strong a predictor of civic participation, it is highly influential for political participation, social membership, and newer forms of online social activity.

In the following sections, I offer some key takeaways from this analysis and discuss some of the implications.

6.1 – FINDING 1: THE CULTURAL/HISTORICAL KNOWLEDGE AND CREATIVE SKILLS DIGITAL LITERACY DOMAINS ARE MORE HIGHLY CORRELATED WITH PARTICIPATION

As demonstrated by my tests of Hypothesis 1 and 2, I find that cultural/historical knowledge and creative publication skills are the most predictive of mass participation. This is likely because of the influence that digital content has on the participatory environment. Many activities in mass participation are increasingly mediated via networked technologies, and as such, possessing the skills with which to be a contributor instead of purely a consumer of information is likely to be valuable. This analysis also found that knowledge of the cultural and historical issues related to technology was a high indicator of participation. Knowledge of technology issues affecting society today, which include privacy, technology policy, intellectual property, and the social risks and benefits of technology appear to greatly inform higher levels of participation. These issues are frequently discussed in political and societal domains, and as such, those who are more attuned to these issues might be encouraged to use their knowledge for participation. Knowledge in this domain also could influence how other skills are learned and used, but additional studies would need to be done to confirm this.

While appearing to be weaker predictors, computer, information, and communication skills compliment the full digital literacy concept. Skills within these domains include discrete abilities to use technologies to retrieve and analyze information. These skills might be prerequisite to learning and using more the more advanced skills digital literacy skills of publication and sharing. Due to the high collinearity between the six domains, additional studies that study these domains individually and better separate out the intricacies between the domains of digital literacy could be valuable.

6.2 – Finding 2: Digital Literacy Is the Most Powerful Predictor of Traditional Mass Participation when Compared to Political and Demographic Control Variables

I found that digital literacy is the strongest predictor of traditional mass participation when compared to demographic and political identification control variables. Digital literacy allows for greater avenues of personal expression and for the effective use of tools for sharing ideas and stories. Networked information technologies provide opportunities to connect with others and organize. The observations from this analysis confirm the argument I present in this thesis that digital literacy skills are increasingly required for mass participation activities.

This analysis is not without caveats, however. While the R-squared value (.067 for the full participation model) is not particularly high, the regression model is statistically significant. This allows me to trust that the influence of digital literacy on mass participation is not just a coincidence: a true antecedent effect is present. This correlation with mass participation might not only be through the active use of digital literacy skills. The mass participation activities of the digitally literate could also be influenced by the training and experience that comes with mastery of digital skills. In addition, this model could be a result of a certain level of attention that is paid to social, civic, or political matters unique to those of higher digital literacy (such as following online news and multiple other information streams and keeping appraised of situations, ready to take action when necessary). Mass participation is a human behavior that is influenced by countless life situations, goals, experiences, and beliefs. While other correlations of digital literacy are yet to be determined, this model can be trusted to show digital literacy's correlation with mass participation.

6.3 – FINDING 3: DIGITAL LITERACY IS MORE VALUABLE FOR SOME DOMAINS OF MASS PARTICIPATION THAN OTHERS

The regression analysis shows that digital literacy is a significant predictor of mass participation in the social membership, political, and online domains. It is not a significant predictor of civic participation, indicating that digital skills are not used in civic participation to the same degree that they are in other domains. Also, each of the domains is influenced at different levels by digital literacy skills. Online participation is influenced by antecedent digital literacy skills moreso than political or social membership participation. Of the three traditional domains of mass participation, political participation is influenced the most by antecedent digital literacy skills.

Online participation allows people to connect with others with like interests, regardless of traditional barriers such as geographic distance and face-to-face communication. As the descriptive statistics in Chapter 4 show, the public is much more highly involved in online social activities than other activities. These activities include networking with strangers over distance, promoting and sharing ideas, forming interest groups, playing games, and even moving from the online world to the offline world for social purposes (such as in online dating and social meetups). However, as the findings related to Hypothesis 4 show, a higher level of digital skill predicts participation in this domain. In addition, many traditional activities are moving into online spaces, such has been seen with online political campaigns and e-governance. As online participation continues to augment traditional participation activities in the social membership, civic, and political participation domains, the study of online mass participation will become increasingly important to this field as people socialize online and use digital skills to augment their offline social lives. The distinction that I draw in this thesis between online and traditional participation activities might become increasingly harder to define as online avenues for participation merge with traditional participation activities.

Higher levels of political participation are highly predicted by digital literacy skills. This can be partially attributed to the increased electronic mediation of politics. With the higher amounts of political and news media that are delivered electronically, as well as a push for governments, political campaigns, and advocacy groups to move to the online realm to meet their goals, a greater degree of digital literacy is required in order to effectively interact. Digital literacy's high predictive power for political participation also demonstrates the possible saliency of electronic governance, political organization, and involvement. Moving political participation to the online realm could make it much easier to monitor political happenings and take action with appropriate tools when it becomes necessary. This behavior would confirm Schudson's (1999) suggestion of the "monitorial citizen," and digital tools will continue empower this monitorial function. However, as the data show, people would likely benefit from digital literacy skills when participating, especially as political activities become increasingly mediated via technology.

From the evidence in this thesis, I argue that those with higher levels of digital literacy skills are more advantaged concerning political participation as it gives them a greater voice to make their needs heard and acted upon. Despite this, American politics has not likely been completely transformed by the integration of information technologies: traditional power structures still exist, elites still hold influence, and those with greater levels of knowledge and access to information are more enabled to participate. While it may not yet be required for a person to have a complete set of digital literacy skills to participate in politics, the highly mediated political environment in recent elections and e-governance initiatives give a greater number of options for people to get involved. This move to the online also might be redefining influence, as can be seen from recent decentralized, online-powered efforts for political change, such as the Tea Party and Occupy Wall Street movements. In summary, my evidence shows that despite the traditional opportunities for political participation, digital literacy skills are increasingly necessary to engage in politics.

Interestingly, civic participation is not predicted by digital literacy. This could imply that volunteerism and community service happen locally and that these activities are not necessarily mediated or assisted by information technologies. While information technologies are likely used to some degree, volunteerism, community service, and active efforts to help others appear to require digital technologies to a lesser degree. This finding can also be explained by the lack of centralization and breadth in volunteer or civic activity. Civic participation can represent any number of activities in any number of contexts, from organizing a trash pickup effort in a local park to serving on the board of trustees for a large nonprofit organization. As such, the manner in which people help others through volunteerism and philanthropy is highly varied. In comparison to political participation, activities are usually organized around a central body (an elected office, government, the news media, etc.) and around a common set of rules and procedures (legislative process, election rules, etc). Many of these rules and central bodies are similar in composition around the United States, allowing for more uniform best practices to emerge.

Higher levels of digital literacy also indicate higher levels of social membership participation. However, while digital literacy is important in helping a person connect to communities, clubs, and other social groups, it is not the only determining factor. The digital literacy variable is joined by the age and education variables, each enjoying about equal strength in predicting a person's level of social membership participation. A person is likely to choose to be socially active within this domain based on their current life situation, such as social activities appropriate for people of various ages, or certain activities based on experiences gained from education. The key takeaway here is that while digital literacy is a strong predictor, there are other life experiences and antecedent conditions that encourage someone to get involved in social activities.

Discussion

The regression analyses that I employ in this chapter indicate that digital literacy is a positive *predictor* of mass participation, or that having digital literacy skills will empower higher levels of participation. However, the paths that people take to acquire digital literacy skills may be diverse and may not always occur prior to participation. The desire for participation and a person's social values, life experience, and other preconditions might influence someone's interest in learning digital literacy skills for the purpose of participation. Also, individuals might use pre-existing digital literacy skills for mass participation when they are compelled to participate for any particular reason. However, participation activities themselves could influence the learning of new digital literacy skills as a result of the activity, such as exposure to new hobbies, tools, or interests as a result of their activities. Future study into how people acquire digital literacy skills and use them directly for mass participation would be valuable to better specify the relationship between the learning of digital literacy skills and the application of digital literacy skills in mass participation activities.

Similar to the model in Section 5.1, individual digital literacy domains are likely to have different effects within the four specific domains of mass participation. It would be an interesting area of further study to see how the six domains of digital literacy skills enable people to engage in specific domains of participation.

CHAPTER 7: CONCLUSION

In this thesis, I explored the influence of digital literacy skills on various types of mass participation by asking the following research question: To what degree is digital literacy a predictor of mass participation? The primary goal of this research was to explore whether digital literacy has become an antecedent skill for mass participation, and if so, to determine what kind of digital literacy skills empower people to participate in various domains. With the integration of new media and other digital technologies into the participatory landscape, the presence of digital skills is increasingly necessary. As such, the primary argument I present throughout this thesis is that digital literacy is now an antecedent skill for mass participation. Those who have digital literacy skills are significantly empowered to participate, and, because of this, enjoy higher levels of influence, social capital, and ability to effect social outcomes.

Using data from the 2012 Technology Use Survey, I presented evidence from five hypotheses tests to support my argument. First, I found that knowledge of cultural and historical technology issues and creative and expressive digital literacy skills were the most influential on participation activities. This finding indicated that the ability to share ideas through digital means and to understand the cultural and historical contexts under which information is shared is essential in today's electronically mediated participation environment. Second, I found that digital literacy is the strongest predictor of mass participation when considering mass participation as an omnibus scale of activity. Third, when comparing differences between the four domains of mass participation, I found that higher levels of digital literacy significantly predicted higher levels of participation three domains: social membership, political, and online participation. Digital literacy failed to demonstrate predictive power only in the civic participation domain. These findings demonstrated the pervasiveness of digital literacy in the participation activities of most domains. In addition, these findings suggest an unavoidability of digital communication and content publication for those who are interested in participating and that digital skills are essential in order to be an effective participant.

This thesis contributes to the understanding of both digital literacy and mass participation in several ways. First, this thesis expands the previous work in mass participation activities in the United States by illustrating how digital literacy empowers participation. The integration of digital skills has been necessary for some time in the literature, but is increasingly difficult with the complexity of how information technologies are used in various participatory contexts and social situations. Second, this work adds to the growing body of literature in mass participation by understanding how the American public uses digital skills to engage with their social networks, with their communities, and politically. Third, the evidence that I present in this thesis suggests that digital literacy should join the several antecedent resources and preconditions that have already been known to predetermine mass participation, which include civic and political knowledge, money, time, strength of ideology, exposure to information and media, and socialization (Wilhelm, 2000; Zukin, et al., 2006; Brady, Verba, & Schlozman, 1995). Researchers and policy makers should consider digital literacy in any future work on participation.

In addition to the analyses in this thesis, I developed new indicators and measures for digital literacy that contribute to the fields of mass participation and digital literacy research. Because of the novelty of the concept, much of the past work in digital literacy has been theoretical. The measures created in this thesis are good steps in the direction of building a body of actionable digital literacy indicators that can be used in a variety of social science contexts, not just with mass participation. As information technologies have continually integrated into the participatory environment, mass participation as a field stands to gain a lot from continued work in digital literacy theory and any subsequent means of measurement.

7.1 – RESEARCH CONSIDERATIONS

The measures employed in this thesis have some caveats that should be considered. First, the indexes for participation in the four domains do not account for the quality of success in someone's participation activities, but instead only the frequency of the activity. We only know whether someone's mass participation efforts were successful or if they achieved their goals, only that they participated at a certain level. Level of participation is a good indicator, however, as could imply that higher levels or repeated activity meets a person's satisfaction and that activity within a realm was empowered by some precondition, life experience, or incentive. Whether activity is efficacious or not is one thing, but with these measures researchers can be confident that a person was at least encouraged to participate by some means. If there is repeated participation, goals, incentives, or other preconditions might continue to stimulate participation.

Second, the theoretical model that I employ in the analyses do not account for some of the other antecedent resources or conditions that the literature has found to be important for mass participation. Conditions such as a person's political or civic knowledge, exposure to information, social influence, or available free time (even when controlling for employment level) could all influence the findings of this research. The model also did not examine the interplay between digital literacy and the other antecedent preconditions and resources that are accounted for in the literature. Studying these relationships in detail and finding how one antecedent condition could lead to the development of another would be a good next step for research. For the sake of exploring the specific effects of digital literacy in this thesis, these other antecedent conditions were omitted.

Finally, there are some challenges associated with building research tools for this type of research. In constructing the digital literacy measures, I was limited by the lack of previous empirical measurement work in the literature. To account for this, I built and tested a list of indicators in six separate domains, which was informed by past work in digital literacy theory. However, there are likely countless indicators and several ways to categorize this information, making this thesis a first iteration of this digital literacy measurement method. I expect the measurement tools that I constructed in this thesis to evolve with various indicators that prove to be useful and more detailed categories that can provide a greater explanation of digital literacy skills among the public. While the literature on digital literacy is robust and grows with each new wave of technological development, research in this field would benefit from the ability to measure new skills and relationships as soon as scholars theorize them. Additional work in observing and measuring digital skills in a variety of environments would continue to empower research like this thesis.

7.2 – FUTURE RESEARCH

With the inclusion of digital literacy as an antecedent condition for certain mass participation activities, future research in this area can further specify the influence that digital skills has on various categories of participation. First, it would be valuable to examine the influence that digital literacy has on participation with other antecedent preconditions and resources accounted for. This research would include the consideration of information exposure, political and civic knowledge, available time, and other life experiences in conjunction with digital literacy. In addition, it would be valuable to see how digital literacy influences or is influenced by other antecedent conditions. Certain life experiences and antecedent preconditions could provide incentive to acquire digital skills, and certain digital skills

Conclusion

could alter someone's antecedent conditions. Future research that better specifies these relationships could be revealing.

In addition to exploring the interplay of digital literacy and other antecedent conditions for participation, it would be interesting to track the specific digital skills that people use for certain domains of participation and the quality with which they use them. This type of analysis could be done through an experimental or other observational study environment. Study in this area would allow researchers to better understand how digital skills are being used, in which combination, and how these combinations influence the level of mass participation and the efficacy of those activities.

Future research should also be done on the relationships between digital literacy domains and specific skills in order to identify the higher and lower-order skills. As this thesis demonstrates that digital publication skills influence participation the most, it would be valuable to see which digital literacy skills empower the acquisition of publication skills. Also, identifying the paths people take to acquire various skills and how they use skills for what purpose would additionally highlight these relationships.

From a broader interdisciplinary perspective, this type of analysis could also be useful in seeing how digital literacy is an antecedent skill for other areas in society, such as the workplace in various industries, academics and formal education, and daily domestic life.

97

7.3 – CONCLUSIONS

The primary argument of this thesis has been that digital literacy has become a necessary prerequisite skill for mass participation. The evidence that I have presented supports this claim in a variety of ways, especially for areas of political participation. I argue that these new skills have been a long time coming. The intricacies of information technology have made communication more complex in many ways, especially in the field of political communication and media.

If we, as a society, desire broader participation and sharing of ideas for the sake of more robust communities, economies, or governments, it might be wise to invest in educational initiatives for digital literacy. As the data show, people with higher levels of digital literacy participate more (especially those with creative publication skills). Through education initiatives that provide people the digital skills, we can encourage greater levels of social interaction and political participation. In the age of the Internet, a more deliberative democracy and robust sharing of ideas could address the unique needs of communities. With the technological provisions of the web, our governance structures could even begin to provide micro-assistance or hyper-local community engagement. Most of this vision, however, would be contingent upon the robust sharing of ideas and expression of community needs. According to the findings of this thesis, equipping people with these new digital civic skills for participation could be a start to realizing higher levels of participation.

Another possible implication is that having digital literacy skills can help people not only be better participants, but also better consumers and workers. Being able to express oneself in today's digital environment can be particularly effective and persuasive if messages are deployed in the right environment and with the right media. Knowing how to take advantage of the benefits and shortcomings of digital tools and the information they contain can be empowering in ways not yet measured by the literature. While this thesis demonstrates that digital literacy is an antecedent skill for mass participation activities, it could likely be the case for other areas of life as well. Gaining digital literacy skills could not only give an edge to people seeking to bring about social change or make their community a better place to live, but also an advantage in career, school, or daily interaction with others.

Appendix I: Description of Included Digital Literacy Index Indicators

Respondents were asked to list their level of competency or knowledge with 59 indicators of digital literacy. For each indicator, respondents answered whether they were "not at all capable" (score of 1) to if they were "very capable / expert" (score of 5). The indicators were compiled into indexes as shown below

The Full Digital Literacy Index includes all 59 indicators included below
Cronbach's Alpha: .910

Computer Skills (Cronbach's Alpha: .924)

Using a computer to do basic things such as get on the Internet, send emails, and make documents
Using a mobile phone to connect to the Internet
Setting up a home network or router to use one or more computers on the Internet
Installing new parts or hooking up a printer or other device to a computer by yourself
Converting documents of one file extension (such as .doc, .pdf, .xls) to other programs that use different file extensions
Changing the screensaver on a computer
Manually backing up files on your computer
Using more than one operating system on different computers (such as Windows, Linux, iOS, or Mac OS)
Installing drivers or software on your computer for new hardware or equipment
Customizing the settings with computer programs or hardware to meet your needs
Troubleshooting errors in computers and fixing them
Connecting and setting up a new computer at home or work

Appendix I: Digital Literacy Indicators

Information Skills (Cronbach's Alpha: .892)

Locating websites on the Internet through a web browser
Using a search engine such as Google, Yahoo, or Bing to find websites and documents
Performing advanced searches or filtering on the Internet with search engines and search commands to find better results (i.e., Boolean operators)
Identifying if a document you read on the Internet is original or has been reposted by someone else
Identifying fake or misleading information, emails, or websites on the Internet
Creating new documents by using or "remixing" multiple types of content (such as text, video, sound, images, etc).
Using a computer to communicate and share information with other people over the Internet
Searching and finding specific words or text within a document or website
Converting a text file (such as Microsoft Word) into another text format (such as PDF or GoogleDocs)
Using a website like Wikipedia to find **original** documents or sources

Communication Skills (Cronbach's Alpha: .936)

Sending emails and attachments to other people
Sharing information, photos, and videos on social network websites (such as Facebook or Twitter)
Uploading photos or videos to a website (such as YouTube or Flickr)
Making video calls over the Internet
Sending text messages to other people's phones
Sending video or picture messages to other people's phones or emails
Web chat or instant messaging over the Internet
Uploading documents or files to web servers (such as, through using FTP)
Publishing documents, images, or videos to a website for the public to see
Accessing websites or social networks on a mobile or cell phone

Sending an event invite or calendar request to someone via email or social network (such as Facebook)
Connecting documents and web pages together using hyperlinks and URLs

Creativity and Publication Skills (Cronbach's Alpha: .917)

Creating text documents with a word processor
Creating text documents with a word processor using **advanced features**, such as layouts, tables, images, and custom text formatting
Putting links to video, audio, or images into a text/pdf document
Creating and editing videos
Creating and editing audio or sound files and recordings
Working with other people on projects together over the Internet
Publishing websites using HTML, CSS, or JavaScript
Creating and publishing a blog or online journal
Finding help from other people on the Internet using tools like message boards or forums
Programming a computer application or program for others to use
Sharing or embedding video or audio files on websites

Innovative Thinking Skills (Cronbach's Alpha: .803)

How long does it take you to use new technologies, software, or apps?
How familiar are you with computer "code" and programming?
How often do you try to first fix technology problems by yourself or by searching for "how-to-fix-it" guides on the Internet?

Appendix I: Digital Literacy Indicators

How often do you customize software, applications, computers, or other electronic devices to suit your interests?
How likely are you to try multiple times with technology issues to make something work the way you want it to?

Cultural and Historical Knowledge (Cronbach's Alpha: .930)

Rules and laws about copyright and intellectual property
Online privacy and keeping your personal information secure
Knowing what a standard or specification is with electronic technology, hardware, and software
The differences between computer programming languages and how they are compatible
Cloud computing and how it works
Filesharing and peer-to-peer networks
Automated malware attacks and phishing
The "bit" and how information is stored in a computer
How spoken languages like English are input and used by a computer

Respondents were asked to list their level activity with 48 indicators of mass participation. For each indicator, respondents answered whether they were "never involved" throughout the last year (score of 1) to if they were involved "regularly / I was an organizer or leader" (score of 5). The indicators were compiled into indexes as shown below

The Traditional Participation Index includes the 38 indicators included in the social membership, civic, and political participation domains [specifically omits online domain]
Cronbach's Alpha: .927

Social Membership Participation (Cronbach's Alpha: .830)

Veterans group
Seniors group
Hobby club or common interest group
Service or fraternal organization
Trade organization or labor union
Sports or outdoors club
School or college club
Local community events, such as classes, meetings, or projects
Concerts, plays, or other large shows
Sports games or events
Public presentations, speeches, or lectures

Civic Participation (Cronbach's Alpha: .838)

Church or religious organization
Youth organization
Parent's association or other school support group
Neighborhood association
Charity or welfare organization

Community issue or campaign
Service in self-help and personal improvement programs
Fundraisers for community groups or issues
Service at community events (such as fairs, expos, parades, or festivals)

Online Participation (Cronbach's Alpha: .797)

Forums or message boards for an interest of yours
Online discussions with people who share your interests
Online games that you play with others
Online dating
Online classes or other types of learning with others
Online causes and organizing
Real-life meetups or events with people you meet online
Shared news about community or political issues with friends or family online

Political Participation (Cronbach's Alpha: .897)

Sign a petition in person
Sign a petition online
Attend a political meeting or rally
Work on a local community project, measure, or awareness campaign
Participate in a demonstration, boycott, or march
Write to government leaders (either online or on paper)
Write a letter to the editor of a news agency (either online or on paper)
Volunteer to serve on a political candidate's campaign
Donate money to support a political issue or candidate
Displayed a political campaign button, sticker, or lawn sign

Displayed an image on your social media or website profile to support a candidate or issue (such as a Facebook profile picture)
Discussed political issues or candidates with people in person
Discussed political issues or candidates with people online
Voted in an election

APPENDIX III: QUESTIONS ADAPTED FROM THE ROPER (1994) METHODOLOGY

Respondents indicated yes/no whether they did any of the following activities in the previous year:

- "Written your congressman or senator"
- "Attended a political rally or speech"
- "Attended a public meeting on town or school affairs"
- "Held or run for political office"
- "Served on a committee for some local organization"
  - Includes types of organizations, i.e., labor, school, club
- "Become [Served as] an officer of some club or organization"
  - Includes types of organizations, i.e., labor, school, club
- "Written a letter to the paper"
- "Signed a petition"
- "Worked for a political party"
- "Made a speech"
- "Written an article for a magazine or newspaper"
- "Been a member of some group like the League of Women Voters, or some other group [which is] interested in better government"
- "Gone to church or religious service"
- "Gone out to watch a sports event"
- Worked As Volunteer In Past Year On Regular Basis
- Went To Live Concert Or Play
- Went To Club, Disco, Bar Or Other Place Of Public Entertainment

This data set is available for download at:
http://www.ropercenter.uconn.edu/data_access/data/dataset s/roper_trends.html#.T4wuEZrOzI0

APPENDIX IV: THE 2012 TECHNOLOGY USE SURVEY

The survey used in this thesis was deployed on Amazon.com's MechanicalTurk service between February and March, 2012. 1180 respondents were collected.

To save pages in this printed version, the questions used on the survey can be viewed on the Internet by visiting my Scribd page where I uploaded the full version.

Link to survey questions:

http://www.scribd.com/doc/96178280/2012-Technology-Use-Survey-Questions

WORKS CITED

American Association for the Advancement of Science. (1990). *Science for All Americans*. New York: Oxford University Press.

Anderson, C. (2006). *The long tail: Why the future of business is selling less of more*. New York: Hyperion.

Barton, D. (1994). *Literacy: An introduction to the ecology of written language.* Oxford: Blackwell.

Bawden, D. (2001). Information and digital literacies: A review of concepts. *Journal of Documentation, 57*(2), 218-259.

Bimber, B., & Davis, R. (2003). *Campaigning Online: The Internet in US Elections*. New York: Oxford University Press.

Brady, H. E., Verba, S., & Schlozman, K. L. (1995). Beyond SES: A resource model of political participation. *American Political Science Review. 89*(2), 271-294.

Buckingham, D. (2003). *Media education. Literacy, learning and contemporary culture.* Cambridge, UK: Polity Press.

Chadwick, A. (2006). *Internet politics.* Oxford: Oxford University Press.

Coleman, S., & Blumler, J. G. (2009). *The Internet and democratic citizenship: Theory, practice and policy*. New York: Cambridge University Press.

Conway, M. (1985). *Political participation in the United States.* Third Edition. Washington, D.C.: CQ Press.

Cope, B., & Kalantzis, M. (Eds). (2000). *Multiliteracies: Literacy learning and the design of social futures.* London: Routledge.

Dede, C. (2010). Comparing frameworks for 21st century skills. In J. Bellanca & R. Brandt (Eds.), *21st Century Skills: Rethinking How Students Learn* (pp. 51-75). Bloomington, IN: Solution Tree Press.

Delli Carpini, M. X., & Keeter, S. (1993). Measuring political knowledge: Putting first things first. *American Journal of Political Science. 37*(4). 1179-1206.

Delli Carpini, M. X., & Keeter, S. (1996). *What Americans know about politics and why it matters.* New Haven: Yale University Press.

Educational Testing Service. (2007). Digital transformation: A framework for ICT literacy. Princeton, NJ. Retrieved from www.etsliteracy.org/Media/Tests/ Information_and_Communication_Technology_Literac y/ictreport.pdf.

Eshet-Alkalai, Y. (2004). Digital literacy: A conceptual framework for survival skills in the digital era. *Journal of Educational Multimedia and Hypermedia. 13*(1), 93-106.

Finkel, S. E. (2003). Can democracy be taught? *Journal of Democracy, 14*(4), 137-151.

Foot, K. A., & Schneider, S. M. (2006). *Web campaigning.* Cambridge: MIT Press.

Galston, W. A. (2001). Political knowledge, political engagement, and civic education. *Annual Review Political Science, 4,* 217-234.

Gibson, R., & Ward, S. (2000). A proposed methodology for studying the function and effectiveness of party and candidate web sites. *Social Science Computer Review, 18,* 301-319.

Gilster, P. (1997). *Digital literacy.* New York: John Wiley & Sons.

Gee, J. P. (2008). *Social linguistics and literacies: Ideologies in discourses.* 3rd Ed. London: Routledge.

Hargittai, E. (2000). Open portals or closed gates? Channeling content on the World Wide Web. *Poetics, 27,* 233-253.

Hargittai, E. (2003). How wide a web? Inequalities in accessing information online. PhD Diss., Princeton University.

Hargittai, E. (2005). Survey measures of web-oriented digital literacy. *Social Science Computer Review, 23*(3), 371-379.

Herrnson, P. S., Stokes-Brown, A. K., & Hindman, M. (2007). Campaign politics and the digital divide: Constituency characteristics, strategic considerations, and candidate Internet use in state legislative elections. *Political Research Quarterly, 60*(1), 31-42.

Hobbs, R. (1998). Literacy in the information age. In J. Flood, D. Lapp, & S. Brice Heath (Eds.), *Handbook of research on teaching literacy through the communicative and visual arts* (pp. 7-14). International Reading Association, New York: Macmillan.

Hobbs, R. (2005). The state of media literacy education. *Journal of Communication*, 865-871

International Technology Education Association. (2002). *Standards for technological literacy*. Reston, VA: ITEA.

Jamieson, K. H., & Cappella, J. N. (2008). *Echo chamber: Rush Limbaugh and the conservative media establishment*. Oxford: Oxford University Press.

Jenkins, H. (2006a). *Confronting the challenges of participatory culture: Media education for the 21st century*. Cambridge: MIT Press.

Jenkins, H. (2006b). *Convergence culture*. Updated Ed. New York: New York University Press.

Katz, J. E., & Rice, R. E. (2002). *Social consequences of internet use: Access, involvement, and interaction*. Cambridge: MIT Press.

Karmarck, E. C., & Nye, J. S. Jr. (2002). *Governance.com: Democracy in the information age*. Washington, D.C.: Brookings Institution Press.

Kress, G. (2003). *Literacy in the new media age*. London: Routledge.

Lankshear, C., & Knobel, M. (2003). *New literacies: Changing knowledge and classroom learning.* Buckingham: Open University Press.

Lankshear, C., & Knobel, M. (2006). *New literacies: Everyday practices and classroom learning.* Berkshire, UK: Open University Press.

Latimer, C. (2009). Understanding the complexity of the digital divide in relation to the quality of House campaign web sites in the United States. *New Media & Society, 11*(6), 1023.

Lijphart, A. (1997). Unequal participation: Democracy's unresolved dilemma. *American Political Science Review. 91*, 1-14.

Margolis, M., & Resnick, D.. (2000). *Politics as usual: The cyberspace revolution.* Thousand Oaks, CA: Sage.

Martin, A. (2008). Digital literacy and the "digital society." In C. Lankshear & M. Knobel, Eds. *Digital literacies: Concepts, policies and practices* (pp. 151-176). New York: Peter Lang.

Martin, A., & Madigan, D. (2006). *Digital literacies for learning.* London: Facet.

Meirick, P. C., & Wackman, D. B. (2004). Kids voting and political knowledge: Narrowing gaps, informing votes. *Social Science Quarterly, 85*(5), 1161–1177.

Milbrath, L. (1965). *Political participation: How and why do people get involved in politics?* Chicago: Rand McNally.

Milner, H. (2002). *Civic Literacy*. Boston, MA: Tufts University Press.

National Academy of Sciences. (1999). *Being fluent with information technology*. Washington, D.C.: National Academy Press.

Negroponte, N. (1995) *Being digital*. New York: Vintage.

Niemi, R. G., & Junn, J. (1998). *Civic education what makes students learn*. New Haven: Yale University Press.

Norris, P. (2001). *Digital divide: Civic engagement, information poverty and the Internet worldwide*. New York: Cambridge University Press.

North Central Regional Educational Laboratory & The Metiri Group. (2003). *enGauge 21st century skills: Literacy in the digital age*. Chicago.

Oldenburg, R. (1999). *The great good place: Cafes, coffee shops, bookstores, bars, hair salons, and other hangouts at the heart of a community*. New York: Marlowe & Company.

Ong, W. J. (1982). *Orality and Literacy*. New York: Routledge.

Owen, D., & Davis, R. (2008). Presidential communication in the Internet era. *Presidential Studies Quarterly, 38*(4), 658-673.

Pearson, G., & Young, A. T. (2002). *Technically speaking: Why all Americans need to know more about technology.* Washington, D.C.: National Academy Press.

Prior, M. (2005). News vs. entertainment: How increasing media choice widens gaps in political knowledge and turnout. *American Journal of Political Science. 49*(3), 577-592.

Prior, M. (2007). *Post-broadcast democracy: How media choice increases inequality in political involvement and polarizes elections.* New York: Cambridge University Press.

Putnam, R. (2000). *Bowling alone: America's declining social capital.* New York: Simon & Schuster.

Putnam, R. D., & Feldstein, L. M. (2003). *Better together: Restoring the American community.* New York: Simon & Schuster.

Rheingold, H. (1993). *The virtual community: Homesteading on the electronic frontier.* Cambridge: MIT Press.

Rheingold, H. (2002). *Smart mobs: The next social revolution.* Cambridge, MA: Basic Books.

Roper Center for Public Opinion Research. (1994). Roper social and political trends data, 1973-1994. Retrieved from http://www.ropercenter.uconn.edu/data_access/data/dat asets/roper_trends.html#.T4usVprOzI0

Rushkoff, D. (2010). *Program or Be Programmed.* Berkeley, CA: Soft Skull Press.

Schattschneider, E. E. (1960). *The semisovereign people: A realist's view of democracy in America.* New York: Holt, Rinchart and Winston.

Schudson, 1999. *The good citizen: A history of American civic life.* Cambridge: MA: Harvard University Press.

Scribner, S., & Cole, M. (1981). *The psychology of literacy.* Cambridge: Harvard University Press.

Sen, A. (1992). *Inequality reexamined.* New York: Sage.

Shirky, C. (2008). *Here comes everybody: The power of organizing without organizations.* New York: The Penguin Press.

Snavely, L., & Cooper, N. (1997). The information literacy debate. *Journal of Academic Librarianship, 23*(1), 9-20.

Snyder, I. (Ed.) (2002). *Silicon literacies. Communication, innovation and education in the electronic age.* London: Routledge.

Street, B. (1995). *Social literacies: Critical approaches to literacy in development, ethnography and education.* London: Longman.

Streck, J. (1998). Pulling the plug on electronic town meetings: Participatory democracy and the reality of the Usenet. In C. Toulouse & T. W. Luke, Eds. *The politics of cyberspace.* New York: Routledge.

Stromer-Galley, J. (2000). On-line interaction and why candidates avoid it. *Journal ofCommunication, 50,* 111-132.

Stroud, N. J. (2011). *Niche news: The politics of news choice.* New York: Oxford University Press.

Sunstein, C. (2007). *Republic.com 2.0.* Princeton, NJ: Princeton University Press.

Trilling, B., & Fadel, C. (2009). *21st century skills: Learning for life in our times.* San Francisco: Jossey-Bass.

Tyner, K. (1998). *Literacy in a digital world.* Mahwah, NJ: Lawrence Erlbaum.

Van Dijk, J. A.G.M. (2005) *The deepening divide: Inequality in the information society.* Thousand Oaks: Sage.

Verba, S. & Nie, N. H. (1972). Participation in America: Political democracy and social equality. New York: Harper and Row.

Verba, S., Schlozman, K. L., & Brady, H. E. (1995). *Voice and equality: Civic voluntarism in American politics.* Cambridge: Harvard University Press.

Warlick, D. F. (2005). *Raw materials for the mind: A teacher's guide to digital literacy.* 4th Ed. Raleigh, NC: The Landmark Project.

Warschauer, M. (2003). *Technology and social inclusion: Rethinking the digital divide.* Cambridge: MIT Press.

Wilde, J., & Wilde, R. (1991). *Visual literacy.* New York: Watson-Guptil.

Wilhelm, A.G. (2000). *Democracy in the digital age: Challenges to political life in cyberspace.* New York: Routledge

Williams, B. A., & Delli Carpini, M.X. (2000). Unchained reaction: The collapse of media gatekeeping and the Clinton-Lewinsky scandal. *Journalism, 1,* 61-85.

Zukin, C., Keeter, S., Andolina, M., Jenkins, K., & Delli Carpini, M. X. (2006). *A new engagement?: Political participation, civic life, and the changing american citizen.* New York: Oxford University Press.

ABOUT JEREMY RIEL

I am a higher education consultant, tech scientist, and educator. I am a principal and the managing partner at Millennial Associates LLC (www.milassoc.com), a consulting company that develops technology-based solutions for the education industry. I'm also a Ph.D. student at the University of Illinois at Chicago at the Learning Sciences Research Institute.

I have been playing with gadgets and computers for my whole life and teaching others to do the same. Fuelled by my love for all things tech, the common theme behind projects is to help others find the benefits of technology use in their academic and career paths and how we can all discover our life passions through creativity and the proper tools.

I research digital technology education, STEM learning, and educational technology. I focus on how people learn using digital technology and STEM principles, how people of different generational and cultural backgrounds acquire digital literacy, and how learning outcomes can be improved through technology in classrooms.

Find out more at my website, **www.jeremyriel.com**, or my blog **www.digitology.org.**

Thanks for reading my thesis!
- Jeremy